Lessons for a Long War

Lessons for a Long War

How America Can Win on New Battlefields

Thomas Donnelly and Frederick W. Kagan

Editors

The AEI Press

Publisher for the American Enterprise Institute

WASHINGTON, D.C.

Distributed by arrangement with the Rowman & Littlefield Publishing Group, 4501 Forbes Boulevard, Suite 200, Lanham, Maryland 20706. To order call toll free 1-800-462-6420 or 1-717-794-3800. For all other inquiries please contact AEI Press, 1150 Seventeenth Street, N.W. Washington, D.C. 20036 or call 1-800-862-5801.

Library of Congress Cataloging-in-Publication Data

Lessons for a long war : how America can win on new battlefields /
Thomas Donnelly and Frederick Kagan, editors.
   p. cm.
  Includes bibliographical references and index.
   ISBN-13: 978-0-8447-4329-5 (hardcover)
   ISBN-10: 0-8447-4329-1 (hardcover)
   United States—Military policy—21st century. 2. Strategic
culture—United States. 3. United States—Military relations—Middle
East. 4. Middle East--Military relations—United States.
I. Donnelly, Thomas, 1953- II. Kagan, Frederick W., 1970-
  UA23.L4855 2010
  355'.033573--dc22

2009050298

14 13 12 11 10   1 2 3 4 5

Printed in the United States of America

Contents

Introduction

Thomas Donnelly and Frederick W. Kagan

The very prospect of a long war is daunting: both soldiers and statesmen have made it their quest to make wars short and decisive. The current "Long War"—which for the purposes of this book means the effort to create new and more tolerable political conditions throughout the greater Middle East—is especially difficult for Americans to adopt as a cause. Yet we must adopt the cause and adapt the institutions of our government and military if we are to prevail. Persisting in a state of denial is no answer; our enemies in this region are at war with us, whether we like it or not. They are also at war with one another, and that, too, is a fact that we cannot ignore, even though we might like to.

This collection of essays seeks to illuminate a number of critical lessons partially and painfully learned in the years since the terrorist attacks of September 11, 2001. The essays were written in 2007 and 2008 as part of a larger project on American land power, but their arguments are as relevant now as then, especially given that the new administration is essentially pursuing Bush-era strategies. In this introductory essay we provide a strategic frame of reference for the pieces that follow. We try to define the "Long War," describe how the United States found itself in it, give a short summary of U.S. strategies to date, and suggest how current strategy may develop. By explaining the dictates of strategy here, we hope to illuminate the issues discussed in this collection, which primarily involve the means of achieving our strategic goals.

What Is the "Long War"?

Many, if not most, Americans are either unfamiliar or unhappy with the concept of the "Long War." The term first surfaced only years after 9/11 and

1

even well after the initial invasion of Iraq. President Bush's "global war on terror" formulation had proved both inaccurate—despite Saddam Hussein's flirtations with various terror organizations, it was clear that removing his regime from power was not directly an anti-terrorist operation—and unpopular. President Obama's focus on terrorism has proved similarly problematic. During the 2008 campaign, he argued that invading Iraq was a terrible strategic mistake that had diverted attention from fighting al Qaeda and Afghanistan, which was styled as the good war. But the Obama team has discovered that, in fact, al Qaeda was successfully driven out of Afghanistan soon after the opening moves of Operation Enduring Freedom (and now finds perhaps a better refuge in Pakistan's frontier areas). What remains in Afghanistan is yet another irregular campaign in the Long War, in all probability one much more challenging than that in Iraq. And the Obama administration seems no more pleased with or prepared for the challenge than did the Bush administration before it or the American public more broadly.

We define the Long War as an effort to create a new—and, by American standards, better—political order across the Greater Middle East. This goal is, obviously, quite distinct from and a great deal more ambitious than suppressing or destroying any individual terror group, but it is at the same time a more traditional and overtly political goal and helps to clarify who is friend and who is foe; one of the strongest (if still overused) complaints about "the war on terrorism" is that it was a war on a mode of combat rather than a particular group or state. This definition of the Long War might also be regarded as a refinement of President Bush's Iraq goals: he wanted a democratic Iraq, at peace with its neighbors and allied to the United States, whereas we prefer to take a wider view as to the form of government while agreeing that many of the region's problems stem from autocratic, unrepresentative governance. As long as the regimes of the region do not reflect the genuine consent of all their people, they are unlikely to be either peaceful or anything more than allies of convenience.

A proper understanding of the Long War also helps place our current conflicts within the larger habits of American strategy making. One might reasonably argue that World War I, World War II, and the Cold War comprised a "long war" to create a tolerable political order in Europe, or that the United States has pursued broadly similar strategies, stretching across centuries, in East Asia or the Caribbean Basin. Conversely, a right regard for how victory was understood in other contexts, and for what was thought necessary to achieve it, can inform current efforts to shape a strategy. This is not to argue a mechanical parallelism, simply to construct a durable frame of reference.

Such a frame of reference also helps to clarify our view of previous American strategy in the Greater Middle East. It is uncontroversial, and indeed regarded as the height of *realpolitik*, to talk about maintaining a favorable balance of power (or a "balance of power that favors freedom") in Europe or East Asia, and to further recognize that maintaining that balance has required constant American military intervention and the permanent presence, if not the permanent stationing, of U.S. forces in the region. Yet there remains something of a taboo against talking about the Middle East in such a fashion; to do so would smack of colonialism or, more mildly, cultural insensitivity. If there have been past failures of American strategy in the greater Middle East—and indeed there have been many past failures, as will be argued below—it might be because we have been more reluctant there than elsewhere to commit to a long-term, comprehensive set of regional political goals.

Two further definitions: of the "greater" Middle East and what has been called "Islamism." Figuring out the extent of the battlefield has been a complication of the "global war on terror" construct; so has figuring out the role played in this conflict by religious faith and the practice of Islam. Each of these issues deserves a far more extensive treatment than this entire book, let alone this introductory essay, can provide, but let us advance at least working hypotheses. The central front in the Long War remains the region surrounding the Persian Gulf, but in varying ways the struggle spans the Islamic world from West Africa to Southeast Asia (and does in fact include, in the form of worldwide Islamist organizations, a global dimension). That this central front is also the home to the holiest Muslim sites does matter, but it is likewise the case that the role of belief has been too often either overvalued or undervalued. Osama bin Laden does not neatly distinguish what belongs to God and what to Caesar. Sometimes he behaves in ways that make perfect, secular strategic sense and that seem to reflect an understandable calculation of risks and rewards; other times, he or his comrades (think Abu Musab al Zarqawi) do things that are hard to rationalize and come close to meeting the Clausewitzian definition of total war. We would simply observe, on analogy from the European wars of the Reformation, that faith-fueled wars can be very long indeed, ending less in victory or defeat than in exhaustion. In sum, these two issues defy precise definition but demand consideration.

How Did We Get into the Long War?

The Muslim world is a large and diverse space. At its West African and East Asian extremes, past local religious practice and culture have created forms of Islam quite distinct from those of the Arab "heartland." America's early economic and military encounters with these peoples was naturally episodic, and it was not until after World War II—when the United States, the inheritor of Britain's role as the "balancer of last resort," found itself with de facto responsibilities for a shattered international system—that there was any attempt at conscious policymaking for the region.

The point of departure for the piecemeal American engagement in Persian Gulf politics and security was, not surprisingly, oil in Saudi Arabia. In 1943—as the United States prepared for the great, global counteroffensive campaigns which were to bring both the European and Pacific wars to their successful conclusion—then–Interior Secretary Harold Ickes penned a panicked article entitled "We're Running Out of Oil!" Though the United States was at the time an oil exporter, Ickes warned that "if there should be a World War III it would have to be fought with someone else's petroleum, because the United States wouldn't have it. . . . America's crown, symbolizing supremacy as the oil empire of the world, is sliding down over one eye."[1] After discussing the postwar order with Churchill— disputes with Great Britain about oil concessions in the Middle East had divided the wartime allies—and Stalin at Yalta in 1945, President Franklin Roosevelt met King Ibn Saud, the founder of Saudi Arabia, aboard a navy cruiser in the Suez Canal. Roosevelt's view was that Persian (or Iranian) oil reserves were British, those of Iraq and Kuwait should be shared, but Saudi reserves, poorly developed but known to be vast, were American. In a five-hour marathon session, Roosevelt found common ground with the Saudi king on the questions of oil development, postwar security, and balancing British claims in the region, and managed to downplay and defer the contentious issue of a Jewish homeland in Palestine. Thus began a distanced but durable strategic partnership between the Saudi royal family and the United States; it has remained the central pillar of American Middle Eastern strategy.

Roosevelt's anticolonialism, a strong if situational strain that resonated broadly among Americans and that was expressed in the Atlantic Charter, reinforced these strategic, material, and economic interests. Roosevelt likewise saw the strength of native nationalism, not only in the Middle East but elsewhere, and the weaknesses of European imperialism. Yet crises in 1946 in Iran and Turkey confronted President Harry Truman with the prospect of a new form of European influence from Soviet Russia; anticommunism seemed to clash with anticolonialism, placing unique burdens on the United States, which quickly found itself hamstrung by competing strategic desires: it needed the energy reserves to help rebuild the economies of its European allies, it had no interest in reestablishing and guaranteeing European or British "spheres of influence" that thwarted rising nationalism, yet neither did it wish to see Arab or Persian nationalism exploited by Stalin and the Soviets.

Complicating the equation still further was Truman's commitment, over the strenuous objections of his advisers, to supporting the state of Israel; juggling Zionism with anticommunism, the legacy of European colonialism, and support for Arab nationalism made a coherent strategy all but impossible. What entwined these otherwise loose strands of U.S. policy and seemed to resolve or mitigate the contradictions they entailed was a strategic concept of "offshore" balancing. This, too, was a British legacy, or at least an interpretation of traditional British strategy that matched Americans' self-image. In simple terms, the idea was that the people of the region would have the primary responsibility for securing themselves and their states, and that the United States would ensure that no outside power would prevent this self-ordering process. Moreover, Americans would intervene only when their vital, material interests, such as energy supplies, were jeopardized; even then, such interventions would be sharp but short, preferably with naval and air power rather than land forces.

This concept of offshore balancing may never have been workable; it is premised upon an inherent mismatch between strategic ends and means. But even today it exercises a powerful effect on the way Americans think about the region and, perhaps more importantly, about our own exercise of power. For example, it has provided a gloss of strategic seriousness to opponents of the Iraq War, those such as Rep. John Murtha, long the prototype of a hawkish Democrat, who argued for an early withdrawal and for adopting an "over the horizon" military posture. The shortcomings of offshore balancing began to appear as early as the 1970s, however, when a new generation of political leaders took power in the region. And the events of 1979—the consolidation of the Khomeini revolution in Iran, the rise of Saddam Hussein in Iraq, the seizure of the Grand Mosque in Mecca, and, particularly, the Soviet invasion of Afghanistan—forced a more thoroughgoing reappraisal of U.S. strategy.

The invasion of Afghanistan violated the first principle of the offshore balancers: keeping other great powers from meddling in the region. Air and naval power could have had little effect on the Soviet blitzkrieg, and the resulting economic and diplomatic sanctions were little more than symbols. The Iranian Revolution not only toppled the shah, once a principal U.S. ally; its ideological nature suggested that the region was far more volatile and anti-American than imagined. The taking and holding of American hostages was a crippling humiliation for Jimmy Carter's presidency. The failed rescue effort, Operation Eagle Claw, became known to posterity as "Desert One," the designation for the staging area where transport aircraft tragically collided with a helicopter, erupted in flames, and killed five Marines and three airmen; the aborted mission underscored the limits of U.S. military posture. A secondary effect of the Iranian revolution was to accelerate and energize Iraq's ambitions to become the dominant regional power; it would take a further generation for the Saddam drama to play out fully, but it was Iraq that provided the enduring spark for a process that has moved American strategy away from offshore balancing toward deeper, "onshore" engagement. The seizing of the Grand Mosque by a small band of Saudi Islamists was even less appreciated at the time, but the violent expression of Sunni extremism (at least a partial precursor to al Qaeda) provided yet another indicator that the old order in the region was crumbling.

The first expression of this shift toward deeper engagement was the so-called Carter Doctrine, which stressed the need to prevent a hostile outside power from establishing hegemony over the region, but also laid the foundations—most importantly, the creation of what was to become U.S. Central Command—for continuing and expanded American engagement and intervention. Still, the move toward onshore involvement advanced in fits and starts: the Reagan administration's failed mission to Lebanon in 1983 scotched enthusiasm for it, while the long-running Iran-Iraq War marked, in retrospect, a final fling for the offshore balancers. The naval operations and reflagging of Kuwaiti tankers in 1987 were narrowly effective, but the larger outcome of the war—the militarization of the Saddam state in Iraq—would have longer-term consequences that continue to this day.

A fuller telling of the Long War story and the deepening involvement of the United States would be itself a book-length tale. We have concentrated on the central front in and around the Persian Gulf, but a similarly complex and convoluted yarn could be spun in regard to South Asia, and many peripheral actions, such as our on-again, off-again involvement in Somalia and the Horn of Africa, could supply interesting vignettes. But an underlying pattern, one that continues through changes of party in the U.S. government, seems clear: incrementally but steadily the United States has taken on more and deeper commitments in the greater Middle East. These reflect both very powerful material interests and fundamental American political principles, and they are central to the U.S. role as guarantor of the larger international system and our standing as "sole superpower." Perhaps most importantly—and this is yet another reason why the contributions to this volume have an enduring value—we do not seem to have an obvious "exit strategy." It would be very difficult now to withdraw to an offshore, over-the-horizon posture; having poked our noses ever more deeply into the region's politics, we cannot easily walk away. Osama bin Laden famously declared the United States to be a "weak horse," but his real complaint is our constant intrusion in the Muslim world.[2]

Which Way Forward?

Thus the Obama administration rightly feels the burden of the "legacy" it inherited from the Bush administration. But the Bush administration had to play the hand it was dealt by the Clinton administration, and so has every president back to Franklin Roosevelt. The situation has been decades in developing; in the Long War, the United States is less like Osama's weak horse than Abraham Lincoln's ox: halfway over the fence and likely to be torn by dogs front and rear.

However, it is increasingly apparent that ad hoc strategy-making is reaching its limits. The Islamist enemy is a global one, and its organizations have shown enduring strength across the greater Middle East. The region's regimes remain deeply problematic; Iran's development of nuclear weapons would very likely catapult not just the Persian Gulf but a broader swath of the Middle East to a new level of instability; a collapse of nuclear-armed Pakistan would do likewise. Old alliances stand on shaky ground, and new allies, most critically Iraq and Afghanistan, are not in any better shape, although the trend line in Iraq is more encouraging than in Afghanistan. Moreover, where fortune has favored American interests and ideals (such as in Indonesia, the world's largest Muslim state, where democracy and legitimate government now seem well rooted), American policy has been slow to exploit the situation.

Nor, despite the domestic political credit bestowed upon the Bush administration by the 9/11 attacks or by later opportunities such as the success of the surge in Iraq, has the United States very much expanded the means, military or otherwise, with which it is waging the Long War. The one exception to this rule is the constant mobilization of National Guard and Reserve units, but that only serves to underscore the core fact: we have only short-range plans for a long conflict. The Obama administration announced, with much fanfare, a "civilian surge" for Afghanistan, and many of its principal architects have set much of the current fashion in Washington by talking about the need for a "comprehensive" or "whole-of-government" approach to irregular conflict. But this surge will be pitifully small, just 400 people, and will take several years to generate. In the meantime, the administration is quietly asking for volunteers from the military to fill the immediate need. And at the Pentagon, while Defense Secretary Robert Gates stresses the need to "win the war we're in,"[3] the White House has directed long-term reductions in defense budgets.

In all, the contradictions in strategy and between strategic ends and means are ever more difficult to resolve. While it is beyond the scope of this volume to divine a comprehensive strategy for victory in the Long War, these essays begin to frame some of the critical questions. The first two contributions center on two key home-front issues: our willingness to endure the challenges of the Long War, and the stresses that prolonged irregular warfare have put and will continue to put on civil-military relations. Peter Feaver, who can claim credit for having imagined the "Long War" trope, rightly understands that, first and foremost, the war will be won or lost at home. The primary question is whether Americans will summon the will to sustain an effort that will be long, wearying, complex, and often confusing. Mackubin Thomas Owens writes about a closely related subject: the often-contentious relations between people in uniform and the civilians they serve. Civil-military relations were sometimes miserable during the Bush years. If we are to ask our service personnel to spend their lives fighting and dying while policing a new American security perimeter, our future leaders must take pains to ensure that the dialogue between soldiers and statesmen is frank and built upon respect. And if soldiers come to believe that victory or the chance for victory on the battlefield is abandoned at home, it might well be that a "Long War syndrome" casts a much larger and more ominous shadow across civil-military relations than the Vietnam syndrome ever did.

The other three essays in the volume address critical questions of institutional reform needed to achieve Long War success. Brigadier General H. R. McMaster, both a distinguished soldier and a scholar, argues that the American defense establishment must see the Long War as it really is; indeed, that it must return to the enduring truths that frame the conduct of all wars. Too frequently in recent years we have forgotten that war is a political contest between humans, not only a dance of technology. We must, therefore, shape our forces for the war rather than try to choose our wars to suit our forces. At the same time, our forces have proven themselves to be remarkably flexible over time. Former defense secretary Donald Rumsfeld once lamented the fact that the American military hadn't been fully transformed before the Long War began, but even those units and capabilities that are Cold War–era legacies, such as heavily armored units, have in fact been quite useful. This is the message of Major General Charles Dunlap's article. Air power—quite beyond "shock and awe" strikes—has contributed immensely to the successes of recent years. The balance and mix of capabilities across the U.S. joint force will continue to be a blessing, and, in war, troops and commanders will improvise tactics not yet imagined. The final essay, by retired colonel Robert Killebrew, advocates a different approach to the question of mobilizing not only the military but other government institutions to contribute to the Long War effort. He underscores the imperative both to capture what we have learned and to use the experience as a basis for looking forward. His argument in favor of building robust frontline country teams also reminds the reader that much of the knowledge acquired in Iraq and Afghanistan was knowledge previously won and lost in the Vietnam era.

Even Long Wars can have decisive moments. The present moment, with a new president, committed to defining a new American relationship with the Muslim world and rhetorically committed to the idea that the wartime decisions of his predecessor were profound strategic errors, might well be one. There may have been a rough pattern to past U.S. strategy for the Middle East, but past is not perfectly prologue, or an inescapable logic. As Americans debate a direction for the future, these essays will better inform them of not only the price of victory, but some of the ways in which it might be won.

1

Domestic Politics
and the Long War

Peter D. Feaver

The Cold War analogy remains the best point of departure for understanding the current conflict, particularly for understanding the domestic political challenges of fighting the Global War on Terror (GWOT).[1] To be sure, the analogy is not exact, and there is now a tedious panoply of punditry pointing out this or that distinction between the conflicts. But within the limits of any analogy, the Cold War parallel has been particularly helpful because it underscores several fundamental truths that were evident within days after 9/11 and that seem even more apt today.

First and foremost, the conflict is not solely or even primarily a conventional military conflict. As the 2006 *National Security Strategy* put it: "From the beginning, the War on Terror has been both a battle of arms and a battle of ideas."[2] No one with any senior policymaking involvement in the GWOT believes the United States can prevail simply by old-fashioned force of arms—invading countries, toppling regimes, and clearing out rat holes. Despite the partisan critique to the contrary, the Bush administration understood this fact from the beginning, and it was a key inspiration behind the "freedom agenda," the effort to promote political and economic liberty as the alternative to the ideology animating the terrorists.

Second, the war will not be decided soon with a single decisive battle nor ended with a signing ceremony aboard a battleship. It will be long and lingering. The military operation in Afghanistan has turned out to be as long running as critics feared (though not as bloody). The military operation in Iraq has been longer and bloodier than most people expected (though some critics correctly anticipated its true cost). The broader war on terror has been

11

far less bloody than people expected, at least for Americans—most expected the U.S. homeland to be hit again. Yet with no end in sight for the underlying conflict, it resembles nothing less than the Cold War circa 1953, roughly seven years after Churchill's "Iron Curtain" speech.

Third, the war is testing American domestic politics just as the Cold War did. The myth that "politics stopped at the water's edge" was disproven time and again during the Cold War, and it was possible to foresee, even in the heady days of national unity in September 2001, that the myth would be disproven again in the fight against terrorists.

The time is ripe to reexamine our domestic politics, and to consider in particular how three of its interlocking strands—public opinion, partisan politics, and the marketplace of ideas—may influence how the war is carried out. Since the Bush administration launched the GWOT, we have completed our fourth congressional election and our second presidential election. The team that has managed the GWOT—a remarkably stable team, compared to analogous groups during the Cold War—is gone, and the new one is taking its place. Just as the Cold War was ultimately won because Americans successfully managed domestic politics in a long war, so may our prospects in the GWOT turn on whether the new Obama administration and succeeding administrations can adeptly execute their national security responsibilities while adjusting to the evolving domestic political environment.

Public Opinion

The central question about American public opinion is this: do Americans have the stomach for the Long War? Concerns (perhaps even doubts) about whether public support would be lasting made a very early entry into Bush administration strategizing, if existing public accounts can be believed. In a September 12, 2001, memo, Donald Rumsfeld expressed concern about support at home for a protracted war effort,[3] and President Bush famously warned that although "grief recedes with time and grace . . . our resolve must not pass."[4]

But it was the opposite concern—fear that the American public would overreact to the 9/11 attacks and demand violent revenge—that may have had the earliest policy consequence. Certainly that fear was prominent among outsiders in the earliest days after 9/11.[5] That fear explains why the decision to invade Afghanistan and topple the Taliban was viewed very skeptically in many international circles; indeed, Michael Howard, the dean of strategic studies and the voice of international conventional wisdom, famously warned in an October 31, 2001, speech that bombing Afghanistan was like "trying to eradicate cancer cells with a blow torch."[6] More to the point, the Bush administration's decision to throw out existing war plans and invade Afghanistan with an unprecedented combination of airpower and Special Forces may have been driven by fear that if al Qaeda struck a second time before the United States retaliated, all hope of restraining American public response would be lost.[7]

Nevertheless, doubts about the staying power of American public opinion likely had an impact on policy as well, and probably contributed to the administration's decision to put the Iraq issue on an accelerated timeline. The administration arrived with the same conviction that many departing Clinton national security officials had held: that the Clinton administration's Iraq containment strategy was collapsing and needed to be replaced with something more robust.[8] The Bush administration initially set out to replace it with a repaired version of containment—with targeted sanctions that would be more harmful to the regime but more politically viable with allies eager to cash in on lucrative business deals in Iraq.[9] The administration may have thought that regime change was a better strategic option, but that option did not seem politically viable and was not seriously pursued. Then the 9/11 attacks changed the administration's strategic calculus, accelerating the perceived urgency of confronting Iraq in two ways.

First, the attacks underscored the danger of terrorists with global reach like al Qaeda—if relatively small-scale attacks like the plane hijackings produced such pain, what would happen if the terrorists succeeded in their quest to obtain weapons of mass destruction (WMD)? One plausible path to terrorist possession of such weapons was through state sponsors of terror who might see in al Qaeda an ally of convenience, in much the same way that Hitler and Stalin overcame deep ideological divides to cooperate, however briefly, in dividing up Poland. With the experience of 9/11 freshly wounding, the Bush administration reassessed all the challenges in the "lingering threats" inbox, and they increased the priority concern of states that were believed to hold substantial stockpiles of weapons of mass destruction, that were known to have connections (however nascent) with al Qaeda, and that shared al Qaeda's enmity with the United States. Iraq was on that short list.

Second, and of direct interest to domestic politics, 9/11 raised the perceived bellicosity of the American public. Virtually every poll since the first Gulf War showed a majority of support for forceful action against Iraq, but most of those polls asked about limited low-cost air strikes. The hawks in the Bush administration had in mind a much more ambitious and potentially costly military venture, one that would more severely tax the war spirit of the American public. Officials were concerned that as the 9/11 attacks receded into memory—especially if Bush policies were successful in thwarting additional attacks—the public's stomach for such a venture would disappear.[10]

Thus, it is possible that concerns about American public opinion helped shape the entry into both Afghanistan and Iraq, the two major military operations conducted in the Long War thus far. What is beyond argument is that concerns about American public opinion have shaped the debate over the exit from those military operations. This debate is very complex, but two broad schools are discernible.

One school holds that the American public has tired of paying the costs of the military conflict, especially with Iraq, and so it now demands that the battlefields be abandoned short of achieving something like sustainable security—or that we "end the war," as Barack Obama put it. Sometimes this school praises the American public for seeing the futility of this war; other times, pundits writing in this tradition seem to be urging the public to tire still more quickly, so careful are they to dramatize the costs, denigrate any possible benefits, and trivialize any concerns about leaving before a lasting stability can be achieved.[11]

The other school holds that the American public has tired of paying the costs of the military conflict, especially with Iraq, but that a substantial share of it is willing to persevere until something like sustainable security— say a democratic Iraq that can govern itself, defend itself, sustain itself, and be an ally in the war on terror—can be achieved. Sometimes this school praises the resolve of the American public for persevering; other times, pundits writing in this tradition seem to be urging the public not to tire, so careful are they to reinforce the warnings of the intelligence community and military commanders about what will happen if the United States leaves Iraq prematurely.[12]

Abundant public opinion data offer support for both schools.[13] As the first school claims, the public's stomach for the costly Iraq War has eroded considerably from the dizzying heights it reached during the spring of 2003. As the second school notes, the erosion has been slower than most in the first school predicted. Even as late as fall 2008, there were not adamant demands to withdraw immediately from Iraq, regardless of the consequences; although much of the public now believes that getting into Iraq in the first place was a mistake, the erosion of support for the war has not hardened into outright opposition to its continuation. Polling results on "what to do now" remain notoriously hard to pin down, influenced sharply by wording, by framing, by argumentation, and, perhaps most importantly, by shifting facts on the ground.[14]

The seemingly endless debate about public attitudes on Iraq has obscured the related but arguably deeper question about public attitudes on the broader war on terror. Here the debate is murkier and the polling evidence murkier still. Some, but by no means all, the disciples of the get-out-of-Iraq-now school extend their critique to all aspects of the GWOT. These skeptics describe the entire "long war" concept as misguided and futile. Fighting terrorists abroad is an "endless war," a fool's errand that should be abandoned. Rather than worry about terrorists of global reach, America should simply put its own house in order. Trying to change the behavior of others is a quixotic task that Americans have never mastered.[15]

However, the most powerful elements of the anti–Iraq War movement have painted Iraq as a *distraction* from the larger war; they promise to pursue the "real" war with even greater zeal once the Iraqi battlefield is abandoned. To the extent that President Obama had a coherent strategy for the Long War when he began his run for president, this was it. Thus, not only are anti–Iraq War leaders promising an escalation in Afghanistan, but some are also talking about intensified bombing of Pakistan (with or without the approval of the Pakistani Government) or warning that if Iran "in the next 10 years . . . foolishly [considers] launching an attack on Israel, we would be able to totally obliterate them."[16]

These politicians are likely reading the same public opinion polls, which show that most Americans still seem committed to the broader GWOT, whatever they think about Iraq. Terrorism continues to be among the top five issues that Americans consider national priorities, and supermajorities continue to list terrorism as a "very important" priority for the national government.[17] Moreover, Afghanistan continues to be viewed favorably, with as many as 65 percent reporting support on the retrospective judgment question, "Do you think the U.S. made the right decision or the wrong decision in using military force in Afghanistan?"[18]

Viewed *in toto*, the most consistent pattern in American public opinion on the GWOT is its remarkable endurance. Despite not catching Osama bin Laden or his deputy Ayman al Zawahiri, despite not suffering another terrorist attack, despite an alarming erosion of progress in Afghanistan, despite a debatable war in Iraq marked by faulty intelligence, sloppy execution, and uncertain prospects, despite a relentless drumbeat of anti-American international critique, despite a parade of embarrassments from Abu Ghraib to the rape and murders in Mahmudiya, despite a cooling economy (the product of a once-in-a-century financial crisis) and a warming global environment—despite all these, public support for continuing the GWOT remains fairly solid. Indeed, both parties campaigned in 2008 on a promise to pursue the GWOT more vigorously, not to abandon it. To be sure, evangelists of isolationism have found a receptive audience for their message, but most of America—high-, low-, and middlebrow—still view terrorists of global reach as a threat worth fighting, and most believe that the terrorist problem will not go away if we simply ignore it. This public resilience is all the more surprising because it has survived the revenge of partisan politics, which (as the next section makes clear) has smudged every jot and tittle of GWOT policy.

Partisan Politics

The issue of partisanship in national security debates merges two fables: the blind men examining the elephant and the dialogue of the deaf. Everyone stoutly describes the part of the problem they are grasping and no one listens to the others. Democrats are certain that, at least since 2002, President Bush (or more commonly, Bush's "evil brain," Karl Rove) exploited the war on terror and the Iraq issue for partisan gain, and that this original sin eclipses and excuses anything Democrats have done in this arena since. Republicans are certain that the Democrats' refusal to concede the 2000 election, even after it was clear Bush had beaten Gore under the rules, violated the core principle of democracy—losers leave office peacefully—and justified anything Republicans did afterwards. Partisans refuse to engage the arguments of the other side, let alone make any concessions. In an era of media narrowcasting where devotees find their views reaffirmed in the rants of Keith Olbermann or Michael Savage, there may not even be a market for such dialogue.[19]

In fact, partisanship has clouded the Long War from the beginning. Before 9/11, Democrats in Washington and in the mainstream media worked hard to frame the Bush administration as illegitimate, despite some modest successes at bipartisan initiatives like the No Child Left Behind Act.[20] The Bush administration, for its part, arrived with an acute case of ABC (Anything but Clinton) syndrome and seemed to go to great lengths to denigrate the policies and personnel of the previous administration—notwithstanding noteworthy exceptions like retaining some of the National Security Council (NSC) staff, including Richard Clarke and Rand Beers.[21] The result was that by September 10, Democrats were merrily cutting off America's nose to spite its face, and Republicans were merrily throwing the baby out with the bathwater.

The initial shock of September 11 brought a respite of several weeks. A couple of years later, Democrats would snicker at Michael Moore's petty rendering of President Bush reading *My Pet Goat*, and Republicans would ask who had a better shot at getting bin Laden, the guy who had been in office eight months or the guy who had been in office eight years. But in the immediate aftermath of the attacks, the nation rallied to President Bush, and Democrats in Congress were not far behind. Some of the key pillars of the GWOT architecture were built during this period with strong, almost universal, bipartisan support: the launching of the invasion of Afghanistan with the air strikes of October 7, 2001; the Patriot Act, signed into law on October 26, 2001; and, somewhat less enthusiastically supported, the establishment of an internment camp for captured terrorists in Guantanamo Bay in January 2002. Though it was not well known at the time, the Bush administration secretly began assembling some of the other pillars that would prove far more controversial when they came to light: the 2002 "torture memo" and early preparations for a military confrontation with Iraq.[22]

The public faces of the war on terror enjoyed strong bipartisan support at home in the initial months. There was the occasional discordant note— for instance, a *New York Times* op-ed by a prominent academic security expert declared on November 4, 2001, only a few hours before the Taliban regime crumpled, that the military campaign in Afghanistan was a failure and that the Taliban couldn't be toppled.[23] However, domestic support was robust compared with the growing rancor abroad. Among international elites even in allied countries, the initial sympathy for America that the attacks engendered was quickly replaced with alarm at what was perceived as indiscriminate bombing of Afghan civilians or torture of captured terrorists (the reference was to the use of hoods on prisoners in transit to Guantanomo Bay, not to the coercive interrogation techniques that came to light later).[24]

It is hard to pin down the exact pivot point at which partisanship returned with a vengeance at home. Perhaps it was triggered by the armchair generalship which second-guessed tactical decisions surrounding the assault on bin Laden's redoubt at Tora Bora.[25] Perhaps it was the reception to the 2002 State of the Union ("axis of evil") speech, which was denounced abroad and deprecated at home. ("September 11. . . does not give Mr. Bush an unlimited hunting license," the *New York Times* editors cautiously tut-tutted.[26]) Perhaps it was the Bush administration's abrupt about-face on support for establishing a new Department of Homeland Security.[27] Partisanship was undeniably in full voice in the debate itself over that department, particularly in the matter of whether the civil servants in the department would be covered by collective bargaining restrictions (as Democrats had promised their special-interest union patrons) or whether the national security concerns would trump labor law (as Republicans had promised their core supporters).[28]

Whatever the pivot point (and there may have been no single distinct pivot), partisanship quickly found a single rally point: Iraq. Today most people probably would misremember the October vote authorizing war against Iraq as a close one. In fact, by the standards of these matters, it enjoyed fairly strong bipartisan support, passing the Senate by a vote of 77 to 23 and the House by a vote of 296 to 113. The two rising stars of the Democratic Party, Senator Hillary Clinton and Senator John Edwards, prominently supported it. The foreign policy "wise men" of the Democratic Party—among them Senator Joe Biden and Congressman Ike Skelton— voted for it. By contrast, the vote authorizing the first Iraq War in 1990 was bitterly divided, with a fifty-two to forty-seven near-party-line vote in the Senate, and with Senator Sam Nunn, then the Democrats' foremost defense voice, leading the opposition. In fact, had the first Iraq War gone badly, the divided congressional vote would have been heralded as a significant omen; and if the second Iraq War had gone better, the strong congressional vote would likewise have seemed vindicated.

The apparent bipartisan support for the second war, however, masked a deeper underlying partisan divide, a chasm that has been widened by allegations of dark conspiracies. For the most part, Democrats have not bought into the theory that the Bush administration knew in advance of (or perhaps even faked) the 9/11 attacks.[29] However, mainstream Democrats have embraced three other conspiracy theories, and the first one partly explains the artificially high bipartisan support for the Iraq War resolution.

The first conspiracy theory advanced by mainstream Democrats was that Karl Rove devised the confrontation with Iraq as a way to divert the public's attention from the lingering economic recession as it headed into the 2002 midterm election. There is no more eloquent account of this theory than the one offered by then-candidate Barack Obama, in his famous October 2002 speech denouncing the Iraq War: "What I am opposed to is the attempt by political hacks like Karl Rove to distract us from a rise in the uninsured, a rise in the poverty rate, a drop in the median income—to distract us from corporate scandals and a stock market that has just gone through the worst month since the Great Depression. That's what I'm opposed to. A dumb war. A rash war. A war based not on reason but on passion, not on principle but on politics."[30]

Democrats were convinced that the Bush administration was beating the war drums on Iraq so as to make the 2002 election a "national security" election rather than an "Enron scandal" election. They worried that President Bush would seek to delay a congressional vote on Iraq until after the election, thus allowing the American public to decide the issue; presumably voters would oust the party that was squeamish about confronting Saddam Hussein and elect those who saw Iraq through a post-9/11 lens. Their fears were not unreasonable. A party activist "found" a confidential Republican Party briefing allegedly penned by Karl Rove that urged Republican candidates to "focus on the war" in the upcoming election.[31] Indeed, even Scott McClellan, who later served as the president's spokesperson, criticized the administration for running a "permanent campaign" to sell the Iraq War and thwart war opponents.[32]

To stymie Rove's schemes, Democrats insisted on an early debate and vote—they denounced the administration for delaying until after Labor Day—and sought to put the Iraq issue behind them as quickly as possible. Most of the leadership did not see much reason to prolong the debate.[33] No one doubted that Saddam Hussein had stockpiles of weapons of mass destruction and was pursuing more. No one doubted that the world would be better rid of Hussein; as even Obama put it, "He's a bad guy. The world, and the Iraqi people, would be better off without him."[34] No one doubted he was a sponsor of global terror, though there were doubts about how closely he had cooperated or would cooperate with al Qaeda.[35] There was doubt about how imminent the threat was, and most Democrats believed the Bush administration was exaggerating the threat to some degree (though no one realized the threat warnings were as divorced from the true picture as they proved to be).[36] However, the existing UN containment and sanctions policy was clearly collapsing, and there was essentially no monitoring of Iraq's WMD activities. Accordingly, most politicians on both sides of the aisle concluded that coercive diplomacy, including threats of military force, was a reasonable way to prod the moribund UN back into action.

Partisan doubts about the wisdom of this approach intensified after the 2002 election, which saw several prominent Democrats losing their offices, in part over national security concerns. As Democrats had feared, Republicans framed the national security issues in the most partisan fashion: as a choice between a party that had no reservations about fighting the terrorists and a party that was soft on terrorism.[37] No race inflamed partisan passions more than the Georgia senatorial contest, which pitted incumbent Democrat Max Cleland, a triple amputee veteran of the Vietnam War, against Republican Saxby Chambliss, who received five student deferments and a medical deferment for bad knees due to a football injury.[38] Cleland, facing a conservative and deeply patriotic electorate, was running advertisements touting his strong support for President Bush's national security policies—

essentially trying to regain office on the coattails of the opposing party's leader. Chambliss retaliated with an advertisement that dramatized the national security threats and pointed out that Cleland had voted against President Bush on national security eleven times; the ad also said that, following the special interest *diktat* of the federal workers' union, Cleland had opposed Bush's proposal to treat Homeland Security civil servants like the members of the military, who do not enjoy collective bargaining protections. However effective the ad was in securing Chambliss's election, it was stunningly effective in shaping Democratic views about Republican perfidy. Interestingly, the viciousness of the ad grew out of all proportion in subsequent legend—partisans falsely alleged that the ad "morphed Cleland's face into Bin Laden's" and that it called the disabled veteran unpatriotic.[39]

There was no turning the partisan clock back after the 2002 election results seemed to confirm this first conspiracy—that Republicans were exploiting the war for political advantage. Soon the 2004 presidential election was launched against the backdrop of a second conspiracy theory: that somehow Rove would engineer a national security "October surprise" and "steal" the election once again. The Democrats headed into the presidential elections feeling fairly confident. Bush's popularity had dropped markedly from the artificial heights attained immediately after the 9/11 attacks. Bin Laden and his gang may have been "on the run," as Bush never tired of saying, but that meant he was still not captured, as Democrats never tired of saying; moreover, at least some experts thought that because of some tactical errors by Afghan and coalition forces, bin Laden narrowly escaped capture at Tora Bora.[40] Of course the only reason bin Laden was in danger of being trapped at Tora Bora was because of the innovative tactics advocated by Rumsfeld, so it is hard to blame those same tactics for bin Laden's escape—but at least Democrats had something to say in response to "Why didn't Clinton get bin Laden in eight years in office?" Moreover, the Clinton holdovers on the NSC had exacted their revenge. Dick Clarke wrote a memoir that excoriated Bush's terrorism policies.[41] Clarke's longtime deputy, Rand Beers, who had resigned in protest over the Iraq invasion and whose warnings proved prescient, became national security advisor to the Democratic candidate.[42] The 9/11 Commission had accumulated lots of incriminating testimony that reflected poorly on the Bush administration, which anti-Bush partisans in the intelligence community were quietly leaking.[43]

Yet it was in Iraq that Democrats hoped to find their electoral bonanza. Virtually all of the core predictions that the Bush administration had made about Iraq proved untrue or largely untrue. The invasion went much better than the Bush team had warned it might; no massive use of WMD, no hordes of refugees, no widespread environmental destruction. But then the aftermath of the war went much worse than the Bush team had forecast it might; the liberation narrative proved temporary (real, but fleeting) and was quickly replaced with an occupation narrative that turned the war into a long hard slog—every day Americans learned of more soldiers killed in Iraq and, apparently, there was nothing American forces could do to stop the killings. More ominously, the search for Iraq's WMD stockpiles became ever more quixotic, and by the time of the election most knowledgeable experts had reversed their judgment on the existence of those stockpiles.

To take advantage of these seemingly favorable (in partisan terms) trends for the Democrats, the party nominated a Silver Star–winning veteran who toured the country with his "band of brothers," fellow vets from Vietnam who praised the candidate's wartime heroics.[44] Senator John Kerry welcomed—even sought—an election on national security terms that compared the two candidates, *mano a mano*. Republicans obliged, and the phrase "swiftboating" entered the political lexicon, derived from the anti-Kerry advertisement paid for by the group Swift Boat Veterans for Truth, whose name was in turn derived from the riverine craft on which Kerry had served in Vietnam.[45] To Democrats and their allies in the media, swiftboating is "a particular kind of dishonesty, or rather a particular combination of shadowy dishonesties."[46] Many of the swiftboater allegations proved to have some grounds, however, and so to Republicans the swiftboaters were simply making clear that Senator Kerry, like many combat veterans, had embellished his heroism and padded his record.[47] Editors at the CBS news magazine *60 Minutes* tried to tilt the scales back in Kerry's favor by reviving questions about President Bush's National Guard service, but the stories proved bogus, based on forged documents, and in postmortems of the elections, Democrats ruefully blamed the swiftboaters for sinking their candidate.[48]

During the campaign, Democrats seemed as worried about hidden surprises as they were about open attacks, hence the second conspiracy: that Rove would somehow manipulate national security policy to produce an electoral boost just before the election. Republicans joked about hiding bin

Laden in the basement and bringing him out just before the election, but Democrats worried about other gambits. "I assume that it will be something," House Democratic leader Nancy Pelosi fretted. "We have to be ready for that."[49] As it happened, bin Laden had an October surprise of his own, and on the weekend of the election he released a videotape denouncing George Bush.[50] Partisans on both sides concluded that bin Laden was simply making a clumsy effort to elect the candidate he thought would most ruin the United States; Democrats were certain that bin Laden favored Bush for this reason, and Republicans were certain he favored Kerry for the same reason.[51] Perhaps the real October surprise was the Bush administration's determination to proceed with plans to launch a bloody battle to retake Fallujah—surely an impolitic thing to do on the eve of the election, but one which at most dampened the vote for Bush only marginally.[52]

It was the Democrats' resounding victory in the 2006 elections that paved the way for the third major conspiracy theory to infect the partisan debate over Iraq. For Democrats, the 2006 election ended any internal debate they had had about the best way forward in Iraq—there was no longer any acceptable alternative to a rapid turnover of Iraq to the Iraqi combatants to sort it out for themselves.[53] Ironically, the 2006 thumping freed the Bush administration to draw the opposite inferences about how to proceed.

In announcing the "new way forward"—which became universally known as the "surge"—President Bush claimed that he had looked at his old strategy in Iraq, concluded it was not succeeding, and wanted now to pursue a strategy that had a better chance of success, even though it entailed new and deeper sacrifices.[54] Democrats did not believe him. Thus arose a particularly pernicious theory: Bush and Rove understood that the Iraq War was lost, but sought to delay obvious defeat until after they left office so the catastrophe could be blamed on the successor (presumably a Democrat). Pelosi charged Bush and General David Petraeus with "trying to kick the can down the road."[55] Even a year later, with the surge exceeding the expectations of even the most starry-eyed optimist, partisan Democrats still clung to that view. As one prominent pundit put it: "We all know it's going to happen. . . . He is going to do what Lyndon Johnson did: make sure the war was not lost on his watch."[56]

This narrative frame came to dominate the long hard slog that was the 2008 presidential primary season. On the Republican side, candidates competed to show their support for the surge and to herald the possibility of victory in Iraq. The eventual nominee was the candidate with unassailable credentials on this score: he had criticized the Bush administration for failing to implement this new strategy sooner. On the Democratic side, candidates competed to show their commitment to withdrawing U.S. troops as rapidly as possible. The eventual nominee was the candidate with the strongest anti–Iraq War credentials and thus the one that party activists could most trust would not be tricked into pursuing a more moderate course in Iraq. Careful parsing of speeches and not-for-attribution comments suggested to some observers that the differences between the two parties on Iraq were less than the rhetorical bombast of the candidates would have suggested, but the candidates themselves were clearly playing to opposite corners.[57]

These evolving conspiracy theories had implications for the evolution of the preferred Iraq policy of partisan Democrats, and this, in turn, as I show below, fed an opposite Republican conspiracy theory attractive to partisans on the other side. The initial conspiracy, that concerns about Iraq were simply a distraction, had the perverse effect of freeing Democrats from devising a viable alternative policy for dealing with the Iraq threat. Thus, in the same 2002 speech in which Obama peddled the "Iraq is a distraction" line, he proposed a manifestly incoherent policy alternative of "mak[ing] sure that the UN inspectors can do their work"—ignoring the fact that Iraq had thwarted the UN inspectors and that only the threat of military force (a threat he opposed) had revived the moribund inspection regime.[58] The second conspiracy theory, that Bush had an Iraq trick up his sleeve for 2004, freed Kerry to run a primarily negative campaign, to condemn Bush's Iraq policy without recommending coherent alternatives. The third conspiracy theory, that Bush was intentionally prolonging a lost war, likewise hinged on a false description of the administration's Iraq strategy, and had the same effect. This phenomenon of tendentious critique paving the way for bogus alternatives merits its own label—perhaps "Bushwhacking" in homage to "swiftboating"—to capture the partisan tactic: Democrats tendentiously described the administration's existing strategy of train and transition to Iraqi security forces, roundly criticized it as failing, but then recommended as an alternative roughly the same strategy.

Yet it was the third and final conspiracy theory that had the most pernicious effect on Democratic policy positions. The logical conclusion to the chain of reasoning that begins "The Iraq War is irretrievably lost and Bush is merely trying to delay public recognition of that fact" is "The responsible course of action is to hasten public awareness of defeat so that it will be indelibly manifest on Bush's watch." Thus, for the first half of 2007, the new Democratic leaders in Congress devoted their efforts to trying to prevent General Petraeus from implementing the new strategy. In vote after vote, antiwar Democrats proposed restrictions on the number of troops that could be deployed and the rules of engagement under which they would operate. The leader of the antiwar faction, Congressman John Murtha, previewed the approach to a political journalist, who dubbed it a "slow bleed" strategy because it would gradually undermine the surge without requiring an immediate cutoff of funding for troops in combat.[59] Advocates of this approach believed that it merely accelerated what was already a foregone conclusion. Senate Majority Leader Harry Reid famously declared, "This war is lost and the surge is not accomplishing anything" on April 20, 2007, some two months before General Petraeus reported that he had the troops he needed to *commence* the new strategy.[60] When General Petraeus gave a guardedly hopeful midway report on the new strategy's progress in September 2007, he was greeted with blistering *ad hominem* attacks from antiwar partisans inside and outside Congress—attacks so vicious that they echoed the worst excesses of the McCarthy era.[61] It was not until late spring 2008, when the surge had unarguably exceeded expectations, that Petraeus was grudgingly given his due.[62]

In short, Democrats found themselves in the uncomfortable but familiar position of an opposition party in wartime. The fortunes of the party and the fortunes of the country were out of synch. The better the war went for U.S. forces in Iraq, the worse it went for Democratic prospects, and vice versa.

This awkward stance proved too much of a temptation for Republican partisans, who took great delight in highlighting it and in implying a conspiracy on the part of the Democrats. Dick Cheney called Harry Reid's assertion that the war was already lost a possible "political calculation."[63] Likewise, Congressman Duncan Hunter claimed the comment had "a demoralizing effect on our troops and an effect of encouragement of the adversary."[64] From such a point it might seem only a short hop to questioning the patriotism of one's partisan opponents.

Questioning the patriotism of partisan opponents corrodes the healthy domestic politics necessary for success in the Long War, but so too do false claims that one's patriotism is being questioned. Democrats have long complained that when Republicans criticize them for their stances on national security, they are in fact questioning Democrats' patriotism. As Fred Barnes has painstakingly showed, there is very little evidence that this is so, at least very little evidence of senior Bush administration officials questioning anyone's patriotism.[65] If flirting with careless rhetoric is equated with questioning patriotism, then there are abundant examples of Democrats "questioning" the patriotism of Republicans, such as when Senator Obama suggested that wearing flag lapel pins suggests a lack of true patriotism ("Shortly after 9/11, [the pin] became a substitute for I think true patriotism, which is speaking out on issues that are of importance to our national security"[66]) or when Senator Bob Graham characterized Bush's Iraq policy as "anti-patriotic at the core, because it's asking only one group of Americans, those soldiers in Iraq and their families, to pay the price of the occupation."[67] Likewise, Democrats are in danger of trivializing patriotism by making it synonymous with criticizing the administration, as if opponents of administration policies are more patriotic than supporters of those policies. Senator Obama seemed to be saying that himself in the remark quoted above. It would be better for all concerned, and especially for the health of American domestic politics, if each side conceded that the other loves its image of the ideal America with roughly the same passion.

The heart of the matter is creating a safe space for vigorous disagreement and debate about the wisdom of policies—and having that debate without undermining the country about which partisans are fighting. This, of course, is precisely the partisan challenge the country encountered and only unevenly resolved during the Cold War. Any security challenge that cannot be resolved within four years is probably daunting enough that reasonable people, and reasonable parties, will disagree on the best policies to pursue. Certainly, any national security challenge that cannot be resolved within four years must be subject to partisan campaigning during a presidential election. The Cold War saw its share of partisan abuses of the national security issue—the McCarthy hearings, congressional Republican goading of General Douglas MacArthur, Senator John Kennedy's manipulation of the "missile gap," President Lyndon Johnson's fear mongering with the infamous "daisy" ad in the 1964 elections, and on and on. We should not be surprised that the current Long War has produced excesses of its own on both sides. And we should call on all sides to do a better job of patrolling the debate.

Partisan debate is not costless. As one Harvard study has documented, attack rates in Iraq are probably linked to the partisan debates inside the United States; researchers found that when reported in the media, these debates emboldened insurgents and attack rates spiked, as if insurgents were trying to capitalize on the debate to further weaken the resolve of the American public.[68] No one would claim that it is the intention of those opposing the war to embolden the insurgents in this fashion. However, neither should anyone pretend that partisan politics in wartime does not involve thorny trade-offs.

In the end, however, it would be unreasonable and self-defeating to expect a prolonged suspension of partisan politics. A more realistic goal is to subject partisan politics to rigorous and objective scrutiny, with all sides being held responsible for the consequences of their policy proposals. For Republicans, this will require questioning the wisdom of Democratic policies, and not the love of country that animates those policies. For Democrats, this will require abandoning tactics that are designed to intimidate defenders of administration policies, such as abusive congressional investigations or threats of special prosecutors.[69] There is only so much self-policing that partisans can be expected to do, however, and ultimately the task will fall to the broader marketplace of ideas.

The Media and the Marketplace of Ideas

The partisan dynamic in the Long War has been more toxic than it needs to be because the marketplace of ideas—the intersection of the media, expert debate, and the attentive public—has not functioned well. The antiwar faction was the first to raise doubts about the marketplace of ideas, blaming a dysfunctional marketplace for the intelligence failures that got us into Iraq.[70] It is true that with a more skeptical media and more attention paid to opposing viewpoints in the expert community, some of the developments that surprised the administration in Iraq might have been more fully anticipated.

The charge (that a credulous media did not sufficiently challenge intelligence as reported by the Bush administration) was worth taking seriously even before it received an unlikely endorsement from Scott McClellan, who as the president's own spokesman was pummeled daily by hostile questions from the media.[71] Yet it probably cannot carry all of the freight that partisans have loaded upon it. With all intelligence agencies (U.S. and allied) believing that Saddam Hussein was hiding WMD and with Saddam himself wanting the world to fear that he was, even a well-functioning marketplace of ideas would likely have experienced difficulty sorting out the truth. Likewise, it is a mistake to equate intelligence or policy failures with a failure of the marketplace of ideas. Consider the Iran case. There is no lack of opinion or public debate about Iranian nuclear ambitions and the best way to confront them. Virtually every plausible policy stance has been advocated and criticized. If U.S. decision makers make mistakes on Iran's intentions, capabilities, or the best way to respond, it will not be for want of public debate and scrutiny.

From the point of view of the Long War, two other aspects of the marketplace of ideas deserve more sustained attention than they have received thus far. The first is the extraordinary willingness of the media to report on sensitive operations, which U.S. government officials complain has compromised the ability of the United States to confront terrorists. This pattern is seen in the willingness to disclose the Terrorist Surveillance Program, the Society for Worldwide Interbank Financial Telecommunications (SWIFT) database, and the National Security Agency database of domestic telephone calls.[72] How best to report on sensitive operations warrants a full public debate and not one artificially truncated with fear-mongering about censorship by Big Brother. Thus it is not helpful to charge, as Congressman Edward J. Markey did, that Bush and the Republicans "have adopted a shoot-the-messenger strategy by attacking the newspaper that revealed the existence of the secret bank surveillance program rather than answering the disturbing questions that those reports raise about possible violations of the U.S. Constitution and U.S. privacy laws."[73]

The issue is not whether the U.S government should be able to shield itself from scrutiny or critique. First Amendment freedom of the press is and must remain a strong bulwark against government tyranny or abuse. Rather, the issue is what norms govern the publication of sensitive information and what level of scrutiny and accountability exists to monitor media decision makers. The president (or vice president!) is not an emperor and should not be above criticism. But neither should the editors and reporters in the mainstream or emerging media. The right approach is for the media to investigate and report on other media decisions as vigorously as they investigate the decisions of the president. To this end, the emergence of a vigorous blogosphere that examines the actions of established media has been a welcome addition to the marketplace of ideas. Blogs like Charles Johnson's Little Green Footballs have demonstrated that the Reuters photographic coverage of the 2006 Lebanon conflict probably involved faked news footage designed to inflate the civilian casualties caused by Israeli military action.[74] Similarly, it was another blog, Powerline, that helped expose the forgery underlying the infamous 2004 *60 Minutes* story on President Bush's National Guard service.[75] And it was Powerline, again, that initially raised doubts about claims in an antiwar diary originally published in the *New Republic* but subsequently withdrawn.[76] These self-appointed watchdogs, like the truth-squadders who meticulously dissect every administration announcement and speech, contribute to the proper functioning of the marketplace of ideas.

This raises the second major issue: the revived debate about media bias. The partisan skew in the demographics of the mainstream newsrooms has long been beyond dispute.[77] Whether that skew in private preferences translates into skewed coverage has been more debatable, though some of the best objective academic scholarship has identified at least some imbalance.[78] To be sure, some media bias is blatant, a fact that was brought home to Democrats when, during the bitterly contested primary, Senator Clinton alleged that Senator Obama was being treated with kid gloves.[79] Likewise, the emergence of Fox, a network that is as pro-Republican as other networks have been anti-Republican, has put the issue of partisan objectivity into sharper relief.

However, the dominant skew may actually be more oppositional than partisan. The media posture themselves in opposition to the existing political power structure, regardless of who holds power. The posturing is self-serving—they pretend that the administration is seeking to dissemble and mislead, whereas the media seek only to inform—and it can be exacerbated when it is reinforced by underlying partisan bias (thus Bush probably faced a more extreme oppositional stance from the press than Clinton did). But as

Clinton can attest, the press will take an oppositional stance even in relation to a Democratic president.

The more profound implication is the resulting skew in covering policy debates. Statements and policy positions of any administration are subjected to withering scrutiny and skeptical coverage. By contrast, *criticisms* of the statements and policy positions of an administration are taken more at face value, while policies presented as alternatives to the administration get a virtual free pass.

The Bush administration was a victim of this tendency in November 2005, when it released an unclassified version of its Iraq strategy, the so-called National Strategy for Victory in Iraq (NSVI). The press treated this document with great skepticism, even alleging falsely that it was not the "true" strategy but merely a public relations gimmick written by a hack academic pollster (full disclosure: I was the hack academic pollster accused of inventing the strategy).[80] Critics of the administration in Congress derided the strategy, and their derision was reported without comment.[81] Meanwhile, the antiwar faction rallied around its own alternative strategy—the declare-mission-accomplished-and-get-out-now option proposed by Congressman John Murtha.[82] The rejection of the Iraq War by such a long-time Democratic supporter of defense spending was, of course, newsworthy and deserved the prominent coverage it was given. The dysfunction in the marketplace of ideas was not in drawing attention to Murtha but rather in failing to examine the proposal seriously and evaluate whether it was viable. I spoke extensively with several reporters from major media outlets, urging them to set the Murtha proposal next to the NSVI and compare the logic, plausibility, and consequences of each. The reporters, each one of whom was assiduous about critiquing administration policy, demurred on the grounds that Murtha did not merit serious consideration. It fell to the White House spokesperson to point out that Murtha was embracing the same extreme position promoted by Michael Moore, the left-wing antiwar filmmaker, but even this mild White House response was criticized because it compared the Vietnam veteran to a Democratic celebrity who had sat in the VIP box during the 2004 Democratic National Convention.[83]

Ironically, that same hapless White House spokesperson became himself the poster child for the double-standard phenomenon. When Scott

McClellan was delivering White House talking points in support of the war, the mainstream media and the antiwar faction parsed his every word and viewed him with extreme suspicion. When he wrote a book that delivered left-wing anti-Bush talking points—without offering any compelling evidence to support his claims—he was celebrated as insightful and even "a Rosetta Stone for understanding the last seven years."[84]

The skew has been exacerbated by two other distortions in the market-place of ideas. The first has been the reluctance of the administration, as noted earlier, to engage in a vigorous debate about many aspects of the Iraq policy. The reluctance may have been an understandable reaction to attempts by partisans to criminalize the defense of the administration or simply a desire to focus on the future and avoid "relitigating the past"— but whatever the cause, the consequences were evident: a stream of admin-istration rhetoric that spent more time restating familiar talking points rather than engaging in point-by-point rebuttal of the critics.[85] The second distortion has been the absence of a "pro-war movement" with the energy and deep pockets that have characterized the antiwar movement. Until the Veterans for Freedom group was launched in 2006, there was no com-parable political action group that had the focus and mission of the antiwar pressure groups best exemplified by Moveon.org.[86]

The consequences of the skewed coverage go well beyond simply wrong-footing White House spinners. Giving a free pass to ill-informed or factually incorrect critiques of the administration means those perspectives linger longer than their own intrinsic merits warrant. Over time, myths that run counter to administration positions become indelible in the chattering class, for instance the belief that the administration lied when it claimed that there were links between Iraq and terrorists of global reach, including terrorists affiliated with al Qaeda.[87] Such skew may even have the perverse effect of leaving entrenched administration policies that a more balanced and nuanced critique might expose as wanting. It is possible that the Bush administration clung to the NSVI strategy through 2006 even as it gradually became unwound because so many of the external critiques—especially those drawing on Murtha's extreme policy alternative—were unbalanced. When the administration finally conducted its own internal review, it found much to criticize about existing policy, but little to endorse in the lopsided commentary that dominated the media.[88]

Healthy domestic politics during the Long War will require preserving room for a vigorous debate, partisan and otherwise, but that debate will be of higher quality and more constructive consequence if all sides—pro- and anti-administration—are held to the same high standards of scrutiny. A well-functioning marketplace of ideas could fulfill this mission—but it has yet to fully be established.[89]

Conclusion

These are fertile fields for ongoing research. Every week, a new memoir or new investigative report is published, each boasting titillating behind-the-scenes revelations or original insights. Our understanding of the domestic politics of the Long War will evolve with the evolving public record. And so I reserve the right to revise and extend these remarks—including amending judgments about who was right and wrong—as new evidence emerges.

Yet even with all the wounds still fresh and the perpetrators still at large, it is safe to conclude that domestic politics will be a key theater for determining the ultimate outcome of the Long War. During wartime, public support for the war is the center of gravity for democracies, and public support is shaped by facts on the ground as interpreted through the lens of the domestic political environment. At the start of the Cold War, George Kennan identified domestic politics in both the United States and the Soviet Union as the key issue, ultimately of greater consequence than any specific external theater of conflict. In this new Cold War, it is likely to be at least as important.

Regardless of the outcome, the 2008 election—the first post-Bush election—would have amounted to a changing of the guard. The actual outcome, a decisive (though not quite a landslide) victory for Obama and a dramatic increase in power for the Democratic Party, increases considerably the stakes for navigating domestic politics while prosecuting the Long War.

From the narrow point of view of the issues examined here, it is possible that a change in party control of the executive branch could actually have a salutary effect on domestic politics. At a minimum, it could disrupt existing patterns:

- Perhaps partisan patterns in public opinion polls will blur now that Democrats see that it is their party responsible for waging and winning the war.

- If history is any guide, the Democrats will find that many of the policies they denounced when President Bush and his team embraced them look a bit wiser from the other side of the Oval Office desk; the governing party simply cannot afford the partisan excesses it indulged in when it was an opposition party. We should not expect the new Obama administration to draw attention to this, but it is likely to quietly adopt many of the policies that it derided during the campaign. Likewise, Republicans will have an opportunity to demonstrate their capacity to engage in responsible opposition partisanship—to be the kind of constructive critics that the role of loyal opposition requires.

- To the extent that dysfunctions within the marketplace of ideas are due to the oppositional posture of the media rather than to partisan bias, then changing the administration should bring some needed corrective scrutiny of the policies advocated by Democrats when they were in the loyal opposition. The media's understandable fascination with and celebration of the historic election of the first African-American president will doubtless extend the honeymoon. But it is not unreasonable to expect that sooner or later the press will begin to hold President Obama and his team accountable with at least some of the vigor they showed in policing the Bush administration. This change could only improve the overall debate between the two parties.

Even if this hopefulness proves too audacious, it is inarguable that the Obama administration will have a crucial role in shaping the norms governing how domestic politics in the Long War will unfold. It took a while for those norms to develop during the Cold War, and they were honored in the breach as often as in the observance. But the viciousness of recent domestic politics concerns even those with long memories of bitter Cold War debates. The country needs stronger norms, and we need them now. It is up to our new commander in chief to lead in strengthening them.

2

Renegotiating the Civil-Military Bargain after 9/11

Mackubin Thomas Owens

From the time of the Revolution to the present day, civil-military relations in America essentially have constituted a *bargain* among three parties: the people, the government, and the military. The goal of this bargain is to allocate prerogatives and responsibilities between the civilian leadership on the one hand and the military on the other. From time to time throughout U.S. history, certain circumstances—political, strategic, social, technological, etc.—have changed to such a degree that the terms of the existing civil-military bargain become obsolete. The resulting disequilibrium and tension have led the parties to renegotiate the bargain in order to restore equilibrium.[1]

There are five questions that lie at the heart of the civil-military bargain at any time. First, who controls the military and how? We often take civilian control for granted, but this raises further questions: does civilian control mean control by the president or by the secretary of defense? What is the role of Congress? What is the nature of military advice? Should military leaders insist that their advice be heeded? What courses of action are available to military leaders who believe the civilian authorities are making bad decisions?[2]

Second, who serves? Is military service an obligation of citizenship or something else? It is clear that the end of the draft in the 1970s changed the answer to this question. But the answer is still evolving, as the issues of women in combat and open homosexuals in the military make clear.

Third, what is the appropriate role of the military? Is it to fight and win the nation's wars or to engage in constabulary actions? What kind of wars should the military be preparing to fight? Should the focus of the

U.S. military be foreign or domestic? The United States has answered this question differently at different times. The end of the Cold War and the attacks of 9/11 have suggested new answers, including an openness to the use of the military in domestic affairs.

Fourth, what degree of military influence is appropriate for a liberal society? What is the proper scope of military affairs? Should active duty officers be writing op-eds in support of particular programs or policies? Should retired officers get involved in partisan politics?

Finally, what impact does a given pattern of civil-military relations have on the effectiveness of the military instrument? All of the other questions mean little if the military instrument is unable to ensure the survival of the state. Does effectiveness require a military culture distinct in some ways from the society it serves? What impact does societal structure have on military effectiveness? What impact does political structure exert? What impact does the pattern of civil military relations have on the effectiveness of strategic decision-making processes?[3]

A substantial renegotiation of the civil-military bargain took place with the end of the Cold War. The change in the security environment occasioned by the collapse of the Soviet Union led to a lack of a consensus regarding what the U.S. military was expected to do in the new security environment. The result was a period of drift that had an impact on civil-military relations.

During the 1990s, some observers claimed that all was not well with civil-military relations in America, and an often acrimonious public debate, in which a number of highly respected experts argued that American civil-military relations had become unhealthy or were even "in crisis," ensued. In the words of the distinguished military historian Richard Kohn, the state of civil-military relations during this period was "extraordinarily poor, in many respects as low as in any period of American peacetime history."[4] Nothing illustrated better the lack of comity in civil-military relations during this period than the unprecedented hostility on the part of the uniformed military toward President Bill Clinton, whose antimilitary stance as a young man during the Vietnam War years did not endear him to soldiers.

Some observers contended that the civil-military tensions of the 1990s were a temporary phenomenon, attributable to the perceived antimilitary character of the Clinton administration. But the tensions did not disappear with the election and reelection of George W. Bush. If anything, civil-military relations became more strained as a result of clashes between the uniformed services and Bush's first secretary of defense, Donald Rumsfeld, over efforts to "transform" the military from a Cold War force to one better able to respond to likely future contingencies, and over the planning and conduct of U.S. military operations in Afghanistan and Iraq. This tension was highlighted by the so-called revolt of the generals in the spring of 2006, which saw a number of retired army and Marine Corps generals publicly and harshly criticize Secretary Rumsfeld.[5]

With Rumsfeld's departure and the apparent success of the "surge" in Iraq, some expressed hope that harmony might return to U.S. civil-military relations. And to be sure, his successor as secretary of defense, Robert Gates, has done much to improve the civil-military climate. But recent events, including the decision by Gates to fire two service secretaries and a service chief and to force the retirement of a combatant commander, as well as a public disagreement on military strategy between President Obama and the ground commander in Afghanistan, General Stanley McChrystal—make it clear that the state of U.S. civil-military relations remains turbulent.

There are a number of characteristics of the civil-military environment that contribute to continuing tensions as the civil-military bargain is being renegotiated. These characteristics, among which the most significant are the degree of acrimony visible during the debate over the conception and conduct of the Iraq War and the perception that the uniformed military has actively resisted civil decisions about the use of military force, are related to the five central civil-military questions above and have contributed to the belief that U.S. civil-military relations are seriously out of balance. Not surprisingly, war exacerbates any tensions that may exist in peacetime.

Public Acrimony

The first of these characteristics is the unprecedented level of public acrimony in civil-military affairs since the beginning of the Iraq War. The clearest example of this public acrimony was the so-called revolt of the generals in 2006, during which six retired army and marine generals publicly criticized the Bush administration's conduct of the Iraq War and called for the resignation of Secretary Rumsfeld.[6] Much of the language they used was intemperate, and some was downright contemptuous. For instance, Marine General Anthony Zinni, the former commander of U.S. Central Command (CENTCOM), described the actions of the Bush administration as ranging from "true dereliction, negligence, and irresponsibility" to "lying, incompetence, and corruption."[7] Army Major General Paul Eaton called Rumsfeld "incompetent strategically, operationally, and tactically."[8] These public charges by uniformed officers, active or retired, are unprecedented in recent civil-military debates.

While there are no legal restrictions that prevent retired members of the military—even recently retired members—from criticizing public policy or the individuals responsible for it, such public denunciation of civilian authority by soldiers, retired or not, undermines healthy civil-military relations. It is clear that many believed that these retired flag officers were speaking not only on behalf of themselves, but on behalf of active-duty officers as well. As Kohn once suggested, retired general and flag officers are comparable in status to the cardinals of the Roman Catholic Church. Whatever they say carries weight.

This public acrimony has been fueled in part by the politicization of the Iraq War. Not even Vietnam was politicized to the extent that Iraq has been. Indeed, one must go back to the American Civil War or the Mexican War to find a conflict that stirred comparable partisan rancor. But this animosity actually predates the Iraq War. Its genesis can be traced to Rumsfeld's approach to defense "transformation," his plan to revise the U.S. force structure based on the purported revolutionary impact of emerging technologies, particularly information technologies.[9] The U.S. Army was often seen as being the bill payer for investment in information technology, and army personnel resented Rumsfeld accordingly.[10]

The acrimony was also exacerbated by personal animosity toward Rumsfeld on the part of many serving officers.[11] Regarding the Iraq War, the central charges in the case against him include willfully ignoring military advice and initiating the war with a force that was too small; failing to adapt to new circumstances once things began to go wrong; failing to foresee the insurgency that now rages in that country; and failing to prepare for post-conflict stability operations.

Criticism of Rumsfeld by uniformed officers is predicated on two questionable assumptions. The first is that soldiers have the right to a voice in making *policy* regarding the use of the military instrument, that indeed they have the right to *insist* that their views be adopted. This assumption has been encouraged by a serious misreading of the very important book by H. R. McMaster, *Dereliction of Duty: Lyndon Johnson, Robert McNamara, the Joint Chiefs of Staff, and the Lies That Led to Vietnam.*[12] The subject of *Dereliction of Duty* is the failure of the joint chiefs to challenge Defense Secretary Robert McNamara adequately during the Vietnam War. Many serving officers believe the book effectively makes the case that the Joint Chiefs of Staff should have more openly opposed the Johnson administration's strategy of gradualism, and then resigned rather than carry out the policy.

But the book says no such thing. While McMaster convincingly argues that the chiefs failed to present their views frankly and forcefully to their civilian superiors, including members of Congress, he neither says nor implies that the chiefs should have obstructed President Lyndon Johnson's orders and policies by leaks, public statements, or resignation.

This misreading of *Dereliction of Duty* has dangerously reinforced the increasingly widespread belief among officers that they should be advocates of particular policies rather than simply serving in their traditional advisory role. For instance, according to a survey of officer and civilian attitudes and opinions undertaken by Ole Holsti for the Triangle Institute for Security Studies in 1998–1999, "many officers believe that they have the duty to force their own views on civilian decision makers when the United States is contemplating committing American forces abroad." When "asked whether military leaders should be neutral, advise, advocate, or insist on having their way in the decision" to use military force, 50 percent or more of the up-and-coming active-duty officers answered that leaders should "insist" regarding the following issues: "setting rules of engagement, ensuring that clear political and military goals exist, developing an 'exit strategy,'" and "deciding what kinds of military units will be used to accomplish all tasks." In the context of the questionnaire, "insist" definitely implied that officers should try to compel acceptance of the military's recommendations.[13]

This view of the role of military leaders is questionable at best and is at odds with the principles and practice of American civil-military relations. In the American system, the uniformed military does not possess a veto over policy. Indeed, civilians even have the authority to make decisions in what would seem to be the realm of purely military affairs. Eliot Cohen has shown that successful wartime presidents such as Abraham Lincoln and Franklin Roosevelt "interfered" extensively with military operations—often driving their generals to distraction.[14]

This brings us to the second assumption underlying the criticism of Rumsfeld—that the judgment and expertise of soldiers is inherently superior to that of civilians when it comes to military affairs, and that in time of war the latter should defer to the former. But when it comes to military affairs, soldiers are not necessarily more prescient than civilian policymakers. This is confirmed by the historical record. Abraham Lincoln constantly prodded George McClellan to take the offensive in Virginia in 1862. McClellan just as constantly whined about insufficient forces. Despite the image of civil-military comity during World War II, there were many differences between Franklin Roosevelt and his military advisers. George Marshall, the greatest soldier-statesman since Washington, opposed arms shipments to Great Britain in 1940 and argued for a cross-channel invasion before the United States was ready. History has vindicated Lincoln and Roosevelt.

Similarly, many observers, especially uniformed observers, have been inclined to blame the U.S. defeat in Vietnam on the civilians. But the U.S. operational approach in Vietnam was the creature of the uniformed military. The consensus today is that the operational strategy of General William Westmoreland was counterproductive; it did not make sense to emphasize attrition of People's Army of Vietnam forces in a "war of the big battalions"— that is, one involving sweeps through remote jungle areas in an effort to fix and destroy the enemy with superior firepower. By the time Westmoreland's successor could adopt a more fruitful approach, it was too late.[15]

During the planning for Operation Desert Storm in late 1990 and early 1991, General Norman Schwarzkopf, commander of CENTCOM, presented a plan calling for a frontal assault against Iraqi positions in southern Kuwait followed by a drive toward Kuwait City. The problem was that this plan was unlikely to achieve the foremost military objective of the ground war: the destruction of the three divisions of Saddam's Republican Guard. The civilian leadership rejected the early war plan presented by CENTCOM and ordered a return to the drawing board. The revised plan was far more imaginative and effective,[16] and further indication that in wartime, the military does not always know best.

Military "Pushback"

The public acrimony that has characterized so much of post-9/11 civil-military relations is a particular manifestation of the idea that the uniformed military should "push back" against civilian leaders when the former disagree with the policies of the latter. This dangerous idea, at odds with the theory, if not always the practice, of the U.S. civil-military tradition, has apparently become more acceptable to uniformed officers, calling into question the military's subordination to civilian control.

Consider a March 2005 column by David Ignatius for the *Washington Post* about who would likely succeed U.S. Air Force General Richard B. Myers as chairman of the Joint Chiefs of Staff. Ignatius wrote:

> When you ask military officers who should get the job, the first thing many say is that the military needs someone who can stand up to . . . Rumsfeld . . . The grumbling about his leadership partly [reflects] the military's resistance to change and its reluctance to challenge a brilliant but headstrong civilian leader. But in Iraq, Rumsfeld has pushed the services—especially the Army—near the breaking point.

"The military is right," concluded Ignatius. "The next chairman of the JCS must be someone who can push back." In fact, the military has recently engaged in pushback more frequently than most of us realize. It is not a practice that can be blamed on Rumsfeld, and it is one that undermines healthy civil-military relations.[17]

While the public's perception of civil-military relations during the 1990s focused on such fraught social issues as women in combat and open homosexuals in the services,[18] the real danger to balanced civil-military relations came about as a result of military resistance to civilian foreign and defense policy. This manifested itself (to use Peter Feaver's formulation) in various forms of "shirking:" "foot-dragging," "slow rolling," and leaks to the press designed to undercut policy or individual policy-makers.[19]

Examples of "shirking" are seen in the behavior of General Colin Powell, who while serving as chairman of the Joint Chiefs of Staff wrote an op-ed for the *New York Times* warning about the dangers of intervening in Bosnia.[20]

Not long afterward, Powell followed up with an article in *Foreign Affairs* that many criticized as an illegitimate attempt by a senior military officer to pre-empt the foreign policy agenda of an incoming president.[21] Critics argued that Powell's actions constituted a serious encroachment by the military on civilian turf.[22] It was unprecedented, they maintained, for the highest-ranking officer on active duty to go public with his disagreements with the president over foreign policy and the role of the military.

Another instance of shirking was the uniformed military's active resistance to involvement in constabulary missions during the 1990s. This resistance reflected the post-Vietnam view, dominant within the military during the Clinton administration, that only professional military officers could be trusted to establish principles guiding the use of military force. Taking its bearings from the so-called Weinberger Doctrine, a set of rules for the use of force that had been drafted in the 1980s, the U.S. military did everything it could to avoid what came to be known—incorrectly—as "nontraditional missions": constabulary operations required for "imperial policing," e.g., peacekeeping and humanitarian missions. The uniformed military essentially sought to make *military*, not *political*, considerations paramount in the political-military decision-making process—dictating to civilians not only how its operations would be conducted, but also the circumstances under which the military instrument would be used.

Although the military's resistance to Clinton's foreign policy predated Bosnia,[23] the clearest example of its resistance to a mission occurred when the army—arguing that its proper focus was on fighting conventional wars—insisted that the plans for U.S. interventions in Bosnia, Kosovo, and elsewhere take into account the military's preference for "overwhelming force." As one contemporary source reported, the military greatly influenced the Dayton Agreement establishing an implementation force to maintain peace in Bosnia-Herzegovina. According to Clinton administration officials, the agreement "was carefully crafted to reflect demands from the military. . . . Rather than be ignored . . . the military, as a price for its support, has basically gotten anything it wanted."[24]

The uniformed military has not only sought to influence the political decision to employ the military instrument, but has also wanted a say in the issue of resources for defense and readiness. Here the target has been Congress as well as the president. For instance, during the first years of the

Clinton administration, the service chiefs for the most part acquiesced in the reduced defense budgets requested by the president, but in 1998, the chiefs changed their tune, testifying that not enough money had been forthcoming from Congress. Members who had consistently supported higher defense spending were enraged. The issue became so acrimonious that "the Joint Chiefs and U.S. senators engaged in public accusations of dishonest testimony and lack of support."[25]

The very real dangers that arise from such a breakdown in civil-military relations can be seen in the run-up to the invasion of Iraq. Rumsfeld believed that civilian control of the military had eroded during the Clinton administration: if the army didn't want to do something—as in the Balkans in the 1990s—it would simply overstate the force requirements. ("The answer is 350,000 soldiers. What's the question?") So when General Eric Shinseki testified in 2003 that a larger force than the one civilian defense officials envisioned was necessary to invade Iraq,[26] Rumsfeld interpreted his claim as just another example of foot-dragging. Rumsfeld's decision not to deploy the First Cavalry Division during the war reflected a similar judgment that the "time-phased force deployment list" (TPFDL), which guided the deployment of forces into Iraq, had become, like the "two major theater war" planning metric, little more than a bureaucratic tool that the services used to protect their shares of the defense budget. In fact the army probably *did* need a bigger force in Iraq, but the mutual mistrust between the secretary and the army led Rumsfeld to make some bad decisions.

Some commentators have argued that relative civil-military harmony has prevailed since Robert Gates replaced Rumsfeld as secretary of defense. On the one hand, civilian control seems to have been reinstitutionalized within the U.S. defense establishment. Not only has Gates fired the secretaries of the army and air force and the chief of staff of the air force,[27] but he has signed a National Defense Strategy document over the objections of the Joint Chiefs of Staff.[28]

But there is evidence that the uniformed military still takes steps to undermine civilian control. For instance, according to Bob Woodward, the uniformed military not only opposed the Bush administration's Iraq War surge, *insisting* that its advice be followed, but it subsequently worked to undermine the president once the decision had been made. In one respect, the actions taken by military opponents of the surge—the aforementioned foot-dragging, slow rolling, and selective leaking—are all too characteristic of U.S. civil-military relations during the last decade and a half. But the picture Woodward draws is far more troubling. Even after the surge policy had been laid down, many senior U.S. military leaders—the chairman of the Joint Chiefs of Staff, Admiral Mike Mullen; the rest of the joint chiefs; and General John Abazaid's successor as commander of CENTCOM, Admiral William Fallon—actively worked against the implementation of the president's policy.[29]

If Woodward's account is true, it means that not since General George McClellan actively attempted to sabotage the war policy of Abraham Lincoln in 1862 has the leadership of the U.S. military so blatantly attempted to undermine a president in the pursuit of his constitutional authority. It should be obvious that such active opposition to a president's policy poses a threat to healthy and balanced civil-military relations, to America's ability to achieve military goals, and hence to America itself.

The "Normal" Theory of Civil-Military Relations

Since Vietnam, most U.S. presidents have adhered to what Eliot Cohen has called the "normal" theory of civil-military relations, which calls for a clear line of demarcation between civilians who determine the goals of the war and the uniformed military who then conduct the actual fighting.[30] This deference to an autonomous military realm is the result of what was long an element of faith when it came to the conduct of war—that the failure of civilians to respect this division of labor was the cause of U.S. defeat in Vietnam.

The normal theory can be traced to Samuel Huntington's seminal 1957 study of civil-military relations, *The Soldier and the State*.[31] Huntington sought to answer the central question of civil-military relations: how does society ensure that a military strong enough to defend it does not threaten it? In other words, how do we guarantee civilian control of the military while ensuring the ability of the uniformed military to provide security? His solution was a mechanism for creating and maintaining a professional, apolitical military establishment. Such a professional military would focus on defending the United States but avoid threatening civilian control.

Huntington called this mechanism "objective control" of the military. It required civilian authorities to recognize "autonomous military professionalism," i.e., to respect an independent military sphere of action.[32] According to Huntington, objective control weakens the armed forces politically without weakening them in military terms. Huntington reasoned that professionalizing the military would render it politically sterile or neutral. The quid pro quo for an apolitical military is civilian authority that avoids interfering or meddling in military affairs, since this would undermine military professionalism and objective control: "A highly professional officer corps stands ready to carry out the wishes of any civilian group which secures legitimate authority within the state."[33]

A more recent case for the normal theory of civil-military relations has been made by Michael Desch, who argues that the problems the military faced in Iraq were the result of ignoring the line between policy on the one hand and strategy, operations, and tactics on the other. He advised the incoming secretary of defense, Robert Gates,

> to recognize that Rumsfeld's meddling approach contributed in significant measure to the problems in Iraq and elsewhere. The best solution is to return to an old division of labor: civilians give due deference to military professional advice in the tactical and operational realms in return for complete military subordination in the grand strategic and political realms. The success of Gates' tenure in the Pentagon will hinge on his reestablishing that proper civil-military balance.[34]

But as Cohen points out, the normal theory of civil-military relations has rarely held.[35] Indeed, as has already been indicated, storied democratic war leaders such as Winston Churchill and Abraham Lincoln "trespassed" upon the military's turf as a matter of course, influencing not only operations but also tactics. The reason that civilian leaders cannot simply leave the military to its own devices during war is that war is an iterative process involving the interplay of active wills. What appears to be the case at the outset of the war may change as the war continues, modifying the relationship between political goals and military means. The fact remains that wars are not fought for their own purposes but to achieve policy goals set by the political leadership of the state.

Like his predecessors, President Bush originally accepted the normal theory of civil-military relations, and he adhered to its strictures until he initiated the surge. But while the president may have accepted the normal theory, his first secretary of defense did not. Indeed, a major source of the friction between Rumsfeld and the uniformed military was the secretary's interference in what Desch would call purely military matters. But although Rumsfeld made some critical mistakes, he was no more wrong than others when it came to predicting what would transpire. A look at Rumsfeld's actions and those of the uniformed military during the first years of the war illustrates the dangers of assuming that the "normal" approach to civil-military relations will always lead to a better outcome than civilian "meddling."

For instance, while Rumsfeld did not foresee the insurgency and the shift from conventional to guerilla war, neither did his critics in the uniformed services. In December 2004, Tom Ricks reported in the *Washington Post* that while many in the army blamed "Defense Secretary Donald H. Rumsfeld and other top Pentagon civilians for the unexpectedly difficult occupation of Iraq," one close observer—army major Isaiah Wilson III, an official historian of the campaign and later a war planner in Iraq—placed the blame squarely on the army.[36] In an unpublished report, he concluded that senior army commanders had failed to grasp the strategic situation in Iraq and therefore did not plan properly for victory; that army planners suffered from "stunted learning and a reluctance to adapt"; and that army commanders in 2004 still misunderstood the strategic problem they faced and therefore were still pursuing a flawed approach.

Critics also charged that Rumsfeld's Pentagon shortchanged the troops in Iraq, in part by failing to provide them with armored "humvees." Yet a review of army budget submissions makes it clear that the army did not immediately ask for the vehicles; the service's priority, as is usually the case with the uniformed services, was to acquire "big ticket" items. It was only after the insurgency began and the threat posed by improvised explosive devices (IEDs) became apparent that the army began to push for supplemental spending to "up-armor" the utility vehicles.

And while it is true that Rumsfeld downplayed the need to prepare for post-conflict stability operations, it is also the case that in doing so he was merely ratifying the preferences of the uniformed military. When it comes to post-conflict stability operations, the real villain is the Weinberger Doctrine, a set of principles long internalized by the U.S. military that emphasizes the requirement for an "exit strategy." But if generals are thinking about an exit strategy, they are not thinking about "war termination"—how to convert military success into political success. This cultural aversion to conducting stability operations is reflected in the fact that operational planning for Operation Iraqi Freedom took eighteen months, while planning for postwar stabilization began half-heartedly only a couple of months before the invasion.[37]

It should also be noted that the most cited example of prescience on the part of the uniformed military—General Eric Shinseki's February 2003 statement before Congress suggesting that "several hundred thousand" troops might be necessary in postwar Iraq—was no such thing. As John Garofano has observed, "No extensive analysis has surfaced as supporting Shinseki's figures, which were dragged out of him by Senator Carl Levin only after repeated questioning." Garofano notes that in fact the figures were based on a "straight-line extrapolation from very different environments."[38] The army's Center for Military History based its figure of 470,000 troops for Iraq on the service's experience in Bosnia and Kosovo, where the primary mission was peacekeeping. This effort to estimate necessary troop strength was inept—critics called it naïve, unrealistic, and "like a war college exercise" rather than serious planning.[39]

Finally, to the extent that Shinseki was correct, it was for the wrong reasons. His focus was on humanitarian concerns rather than on the critical society-building work that the U.S. military had to implement in Iraq.[40] Garofano concludes that the oft-made charge against Rumsfeld— he punished Shinseki for "being right"—is not supported by the evidence. War planning "comes down, as it did in Vietnam, to analysis, getting it right, and providing clear alternatives that address or confront policy goals."[41] This the uniformed military in general and Shinseki in particular failed to do.

As these incidents make clear, adherence to the normal theory of civil-military relations does not necessarily guarantee the best outcome, and President Bush finally abandoned his commitment to the normal theory. The process began in January 2007, when the president announced the Iraq War surge, changing secretaries of defense and replacing the generals responsible for the actual conduct of operations. To an extent unmatched since Abraham Lincoln issued the Emancipation Proclamation during the Civil War, President Bush assumed responsibility for the strategy and conduct of the war. He continued the process when he nominated David Petraeus as the commander of U.S. Central Command.

Of course, his critics assailed him for replacing generals who disagreed with his approach with yes-men. But President Bush did nothing more than Abraham Lincoln did when he sacked generals who were not performing to a standard required for Union victory. When it became clear to Lincoln in fall 1862 that Major General George B. McClellan did not accept the strategy of striking at the heart of the Confederacy's social system— indeed, that he was undermining it—Lincoln relieved McClellan of his command. While the Emancipation Proclamation made the Civil War Lincoln's war, it was not until early 1864 that he found the general who would take all the steps necessary to win it—Ulysses S. Grant.

By taking control of the conduct of the war and promoting generals who shared his vision, Lincoln ultimately crushed the rebellion and saved the Union. In January 2007, President Bush replicated Lincoln's approach in Iraq. His elevation of Petraeus to head U.S. Central Command indicated that Bush had found his Grant.

Overwhelmingly confirmed by the Senate on July 10, 2008, General Petraeus replaced Admiral William Fallon, who was given to McClellan-like public pronouncements. Just as Lincoln bet that Grant could replicate his earlier successes at Vicksburg and Chattanooga and achieve the final defeat of the Confederacy, Bush bet that General Petraeus would be able to replicate his Iraq success at the theater level, a level that includes operations in Afghanistan as well as Iraq.

Civil-Military Relations and the Constraints of Service Culture

With the end of the Cold War, each of the services struggled to redefine its respective "strategic concept," which according to Samuel Huntington constitutes "the fundamental element of a military service," the basic "statement of [its] role . . . or purpose in implementing national policy."[42] A clear strategic concept is critical to the ability of a service to organize and employ the resources that Congress allocates to it.

It also largely determines a service's organizational culture. Some years ago, the late Carl Builder of Rand wrote a book called *The Masks of War*, in which he demonstrated the importance of the organizational cultures of the various military services in creating differing "personalities," identities, and behaviors.[43] His point was that each service possesses a preferred way of fighting and that "the unique service identities . . . are likely to persist for a very long time."[44]

The organizational culture of a service in turn exerts a strong influence on civil-military relations, frequently constraining what civilian leaders can do and often constituting an obstacle to change and innovation. Despite the passage of the Goldwater-Nichols Department of Defense Reorganization Act of 1986, which revised and simplified the military command structure, service cultures persist, with implications for civil-military relations. At issue here is the fifth question broached at the outset of this essay: what impact does a given pattern of civil-military relations have on the effectiveness of the military instrument? And who decides whether the military instrument is effective, the civilian policymakers or the military itself?

An illuminating illustration of this phenomenon at work has been the recent attempt to institutionalize counterinsurgency doctrine within the U.S. Army, a difficult task, given the army's preference for fighting large-scale conventional war—despite the fact that throughout most of its existence, the conflicts in which the U.S. Army engaged were actually irregular wars. Most of this constabulary work was domestic, the Indian Wars representing the most important case. But the U.S. Army also successfully executed constabulary operations in the Philippines after the Spanish-American War, which involved both nation building and counterinsurgency.[45]

Notwithstanding this history, the U.S. Army's strategic concept and the resulting organizational culture have emphasized "big wars" over irregular warfare and constabulary missions. This preference owes much to the influence of Emory Upton, an innovative officer with an outstanding Civil War record.[46] An 1861 graduate of West Point, he was a brevet brigadier general by the end of the war and later became a protégé of William Tecumseh Sherman. When Sherman became general in chief of the army, he sent Upton around the world as a military observer.

Upton believed the constabulary focus was outdated. He was especially impressed by Prussian military policy, Prussia's ability to conduct war against the armies of other military powers, and its emphasis on professionalism. Certainly Prussia's overwhelming successes against Denmark, Austria, and France in the Wars of German Unification (1864–71) made the Prussian army the new exemplar of military excellence in Europe.

Upon his return to the United States, Upton proposed a number of radical reforms, including abandoning the citizen-soldier model and relying instead on a professional soldiery, reducing civilian "interference" in military affairs, and deemphasizing the constabulary operations that had characterized the army's role during most of the nineteenth century—with the exception of the Mexican War and the Civil War—in favor of preparing for a potential conflict with a foreign enemy.[47] Given the tenor of the time, all of his proposals were rejected. In ill health, Upton resigned from the army and in 1881 committed suicide.

But the triumph of Progressivism, a political program that valued scientific expertise and professionalism, the end of the army's constabulary duties on the western frontier, and the problems associated with mobilizing for and fighting the Spanish-American War made Upton's proposed reforms more attractive, especially within the army's officer corps. In 1904, Secretary of War Elihu Root published Upton's *Military Policy of the United States*. While many of Upton's more radical proposals remained unacceptable to republican America, the idea of reorienting the army away from constabulary duties toward defeat of other states' conventional forces caught on.

While the army returned to constabulary duties after World War I, Upton's spirit now permeated the professional army culture. World War II vindicated Upton's vision, and his view continued to govern U.S. army thinking throughout the Cold War. In Vietnam, especially under the command of General William Westmoreland, it remained dominant—and problematic.

Westmoreland's operational strategy emphasized the attrition of the forces of the People's Army of Vietnam: it relied on multibattalion, and sometimes even multidivision, sweeps to find and destroy the enemy with superior firepower. Westmoreland emphasized the destruction of enemy forces instead of seeking to control key areas in order to protect the South Vietnamese population. Unfortunately, such search-and-destroy operations were generally unsuccessful—the enemy could usually avoid battle unless it was advantageous for him to accept it—and they were costly both to the American soldiers who conducted them and the Vietnamese civilians in the area. In addition, General Westmoreland ignored the insurgency and pushed the South Vietnamese aside.

When General Creighton Abrams replaced General Westmoreland as overall U.S. commander shortly after the Tet Offensive, he adopted a new approach—one similar to that of the marines—that came close to winning the war. He emphasized protection of the South Vietnamese population by controlling key areas rather than the destruction of enemy forces per se. He then concentrated on attacking the enemy's prepositioned supplies, which disrupted North Vietnamese offensive timetables and bought more time for Vietnamization, the plan under which the South Vietnamese would assume a greater role as the Americans began to withdraw. Finally, rather than ignoring the insurgency and pushing the South Vietnamese aside, as General Westmoreland had done, General Abrams followed a policy of "one war," integrating all aspects of the struggle against the Communists.[48]

But despite an improved security situation from 1969 to 1974, Congress ended support for South Vietnam, Saigon fell, and the army, badly hurt by the war, concluded that it should avoid such "irregular" conflicts in the future. In the 1970s, the army discarded what doctrine for small wars and counterinsurgency it had developed in Vietnam, choosing once again to focus on big wars.

But Iraq and Afghanistan prove that we don't always get to fight the wars we want—and that the service branches must be able to function beyond the preferences dictated by their respective cultures. While the army must continue to plan to fight conventional wars, it must also—given the likelihood that future adversaries will seek to avoid our conventional advantage—be able to fight irregular wars. General Petraeus's success in Iraq indicates that the army has begun the necessary transformation. The question, of course, is whether the army will internalize these lessons, something Emory Upton's army has resisted in the past.

In a blistering critique of U.S. Army leadership in the April 2007 issue of *Armed Forces Journal*, army lieutenant colonel Paul Yingling wrote:

> For the second time in a generation, the United States faces the prospect of defeat at the hands of an insurgency. In April 1975, the U.S. fled the Republic of Vietnam, abandoning our allies to their fate at the hands of North Vietnamese communists. In

2007, Iraq's grave and deteriorating condition offers diminishing hope for an American victory and portends risk of an even wider and more destructive regional war.

These debacles are not attributable to individual failures, but rather to a crisis in an entire institution: America's general officer corps. America's generals have repeated the mistakes of Vietnam in Iraq. First, throughout the 1990s our generals failed to envision the conditions of future combat and prepare their forces accordingly. Second, America's generals failed to estimate correctly both the means and the ways necessary to achieve the aims of policy prior to beginning the war in Iraq. Finally, America's generals did not provide Congress and the public with an accurate assessment of the conflict in Iraq.[49]

This critique is common among junior army officers, but there are indications that it is being voiced at higher levels, and in particular that Secretary Gates is keen to address the problem. Significantly, he has attempted to institutionalize a small-wars/counterinsurgency mind-set by placing the army's promotion policy in the hands of General Petraeus and those who share his view.[50] Of course, the budgets of the services—what they recognize as priorities—will also provide evidence concerning the degree to which they have adapted to new circumstances.

There are other ways in which the culture of a service constrains civilian leaders, renders military leaders resistant to change, and hence influences civil-military relations. Consider the heated debate currently raging concerning the shape of the future U.S. Army.[51] The "crusaders"—advocates of the "Long War," argue that Iraq and Afghanistan are characteristic of the protracted and ambiguous wars America will fight in the future. Accordingly, they say, the army should be developing a force designed to fight the Long War on terrorism, primarily by preparing for "small wars" and insurgencies. The "traditionalists" or "conservatives" concede that irregular warfare will occur more frequently in the future than interstate war. But they conclude that such conflicts do not threaten U.S. strategic interests in the way large-scale conflicts do. They fear that the Long War school's focus on small wars and insurgencies will transform the army into a constabulary force, whose enhanced capability for conducting stability operations and nation building would be purchased at a high cost: the ability to conduct large-scale conventional war.

The outcome of this debate has implications for both national security policy and civil-military relations. It raises two related questions: given its global role, can the United States afford to choose only one path for its military? And to what extent should military decisions constrain policy and strategy questions that lie within the purview of civilian authorities? In other words, can military doctrine and force structure be left strictly to the military?

Constraints on executive power may very well be a good and necessary thing, but it is not up to the army—or any other uniformed military service—to decide on what these constraints should be. If the traditionalists are indeed seeking to constrain the executive by limiting the use of U.S. military power by de-emphasizing the capabilities necessary for waging small wars, they are wrong to do so.

By law, the services are responsible for organizing, training, and equipping their units and for developing doctrine, i.e., determining how to fight. But the services owe civilian leaders an instrument that is capable of advancing U.S. interests against threats that may occur across the entire spectrum of conflict. Healthy civil-military relations make such an instrument possible.

The Unintended Consequences of Defense Reform

It is now over two decades since the passage of the Goldwater-Nichols Department of Defense Reorganization Act of 1986. Goldwater-Nichols was the culmination of a defense unification process that began before the end of World War II but that accelerated during the early 1980s. Congress was roused to action by the confluence of three factors: perceived military failures (or at most, marginal successes) stretching from the Vietnam War to Operation Eagle Claw (sometimes called Desert One), the Iran hostage rescue, the Beirut bombing, and Grenada; public criticism of the existing defense structure by high-ranking officials; and critiques by respected defense analysts and think tanks. Both houses of Congress began a process of investigations and hearings expected to culminate in legislation calling for substantial changes in the Department of Defense.

For the most part, the effects of Goldwater-Nichols have been positive, but there have been several unintended consequences of the act that affect civil-military relations. The most important of these has been to increase the power of the combatant commanders, in effect establishing regional pro-consuls with vast powers that exceed those of military officers in the past.

In passing Goldwater-Nichols, Congress sought to address two central concerns: 1) the excessive power and influence of the separate services; and 2) the mismatch between the authority of the combatant commanders and their responsibilities. On the one hand, congressional reformers believed that the influence of the four services was out of proportion to their legally assigned and limited formal responsibilities, making it difficult, if not impossible, to integrate the separate capabilities of service components into effective units capable of the joint operations called for in modern war. On the other hand, while a major goal of the Department of Defense Reorganization Act of 1958 had been to create truly unified combatant commands, "singly led and prepared to fight as one, regardless of service," this provision was more honored in the breach than in the observance. In 1970, a Blue Ribbon Defense Panel established by President Richard Nixon found that "'unification' of either command or the forces is more cosmetic than substantive."[52] Goldwater-Nichols rectified this problem by specifying in detail the command authority of the combatant commanders and by placing the bulk of U.S. armed forces under the commanders' authority.

But while it is arguable that the quality of military operations has improved since the passage of Goldwater-Nichols, the power of regional combatant commanders constitutes a challenge to balanced civil-military relations. A recent case in point is that of Admiral William Fallon, who saw it as part of his job to repeatedly and publicly criticize the Bush administration's Iran policy.

On March 11, 2008, Fallon, commander of U.S. Central Command—a regional combatant command that includes Iraq and Iran—stepped down from his post, offering as his reason the public "misperception" that he had disagreed with the Bush administration over policy in the Middle East, especially with regard to Iran. In a letter to Secretary of Defense Robert Gates, Fallon wrote that "the current embarrassing situation and public perception of differences between my views and administration policy and the distraction this causes from the mission make this the right thing to do."[53]

The proximate cause of Fallon's departure was an article by Thomas Barnett in the April 2008 issue of *Esquire*. Entitled "The Man Between War and Peace," the piece began: "As head of U.S. Central Command, Admiral William 'Fox' Fallon is in charge of American military strategy for the most troubled parts of the world. Now, as the White House has been escalating the war of words with Iran, and seeming ever more determined to strike militarily before the end of this presidency, the admiral has urged restraint and diplomacy. Who will prevail, the president or the admiral?"[54]

Barnett portrayed Fallon as "brazenly challenging" President Bush on Iran, pushing back "against what he saw as an ill-advised action." Certainly reasonable people can disagree over the wisdom of the Bush administration's Iran policy; what is troubling is the extent to which a combatant commander took it on himself to develop and disseminate policy independently of the president. Doing so flies in the face of conventions governing American civil-military relations that go back to the American Revolution.

Claims to the contrary notwithstanding, the differences between Fallon and the administration were real, not the result of any misperception. It is well established that Fallon worked to undermine the surge in Iraq by pushing for faster troop reductions than the commander on the ground in Iraq, General David Petraeus, thought prudent. He attempted to banish the phrase "the Long War" because, according to Barnett, it "signaled a long haul that Fallon simply finds unacceptable."

Fallon also undercut the cornerstone of the Bush administration's Iran policy, which holds that all options, including the use of military force, must be kept open in order to pressure Iran to forgo its nuclear ambitions. Bush's policy makes diplomatic sense. As Frederick the Great once observed, diplomacy without force is like music without instruments. But in November of 2008, Fallon told Al Jazeera TV, "This constant drumbeat of conflict . . . is not helpful and not useful. I expect that there will be no war, and that is what we ought to be working for. We ought to try to do our utmost to create different conditions."[55] And before a trip to Egypt during the same month, Fallon told the *Financial Times* that a military strike against Iran was not "in the offing. Another war is just not where we want to go."[56]

It is thus undeniable that as chief of Central Command, Fallon exceeded his authority.[57] Fallon's public pronouncements were in stark contrast to statements by other high-ranking military officers who—whatever their views of going to war with Iran while the U.S. military is heavily engaged in Iraq and Afghanistan—have not attempted, even indirectly, to constrain American foreign policy to the extent that Fallon has. Indeed, had Fallon not stepped down, the president would have been perfectly justified in firing him, as Abraham Lincoln fired Major General George B. McClellan, as Franklin Roosevelt fired Rear Admiral James O. Richardson, and as Harry Truman fired General Douglas MacArthur.[58]

The problem wasn't that Fallon was merely "pushing back" within the administration against a policy he didn't like. The problem was that a uniformed officer was actively working to undermine that policy after the decision had been made—that he was speaking out against the policy publicly while being charged with executing it. The playing field is not level for commanders speaking in public. They have a responsibility to support the missions they've been given, not to publicly evaluate the wisdom of the policy; among other things, such a public evaluation undermines the confidence of their subordinates as they go into battle.

The cornerstone of U.S. civil-military relations is simple and straightforward: the uniformed military is expected to provide its best advice to civil authorities, who alone are responsible for policy. While the wisdom of military action against Iran or any other adversary can always be debated, the decision to take such action lies with civilian authorities, not with a military commander.

Most American military commanders have understood this. For instance, according to Dana Priest's book *The Mission*, the Clinton White House wanted U.S. pilots in the no-fly zone to provoke the Iraqis into attacking American planes.[59] The head of Central Command at the time, General Anthony Zinni, believed that this could lead to war with Iraq and insisted that the White House issue him a direct order to undertake such an action. Faced with leaving a paper trail, the White House changed its mind.

General George Marshall offers an even more compelling model for civil-military balance: military leaders must inform civil leaders if they have reservations about a proposed policy—but they must put doubts aside once the policy is decided on. As Secretary Gates explained in an address at the U.S. Military Academy,

> The Germans [in mid-1940] had just overrun France and the battle of Britain was about to begin. FDR believed that rushing

arms and equipment to Britain, including half of America's bomber production, should be the top priority in order to save our ally. Marshall believed that rearming America should come first. Roosevelt overruled Marshall and others, and came down on what most historians believe is the correct decision—to do what was necessary to keep England alive.

The significant thing is what did *not* happen next. There was a powerful domestic constituency for Marshall's position among a whole host of newspapers and congressmen and lobbies, and yet Marshall did not exploit and use them. There were no overtures to friendly congressional committee chairmen, no leaks to sympathetic reporters, no ghostwritten editorials in newspapers, no coalition-building with advocacy groups. Marshall and his colleagues made the policy work and kept England alive.[60]

The Marshall case illustrates that uniformed officers have an obligation to stand up to civilian leaders if they think a policy is flawed. They must convey their concerns to civilian policymakers forcefully and truthfully. If they believe the door is closed to them at the Pentagon or the White House, they also have access to Congress. But once a policy decision is made, soldiers are obligated to carry it out to the best of their ability, whether their advice is heeded or not.[61]

Unfortunately, the power of a theater combatant commander, which exceeds that of just about every civilian in government except the president and secretary of defense, makes it tempting for him go beyond implementing policy to presuming to make it. Those who do presume, especially in public, pose a danger to civil-military relations, and to republican government.

A second defense reorganization measure with significant implications for civil-military relations was the establishment of U.S. Special Operations Command. Galled by the failure of Operation Eagle Claw, the attempt to rescue U.S. hostages at the American Embassy in Tehran, reformers in Congress agitated for changes that would improve the performance of U.S. Special Operations Forces and raise their status within the department. Congress sought, among other goals, to provide close civilian oversight for special operations and low-intensity conflict activities; to ensure that genuine expertise and a diversity of views were available to the president and secretary of defense regarding special operations requirements and low-intensity threats; to improve interagency planning and coordination for special operations and low-intensity conflict; and to bolster special operations capabilities in such areas as joint doctrine and training, intelligence support, command and control, budgetary authority, personnel management, and mission planning.[62]

Despite substantial resistance on the part of the Pentagon, both the House and Senate passed reform bills for Special Operations Forces in 1986. The reconciled bill amended the Goldwater-Nichols Act by establishing a unified Special Operations Command for the Special Operations Forces of all services, headed by a four-star general or admiral, an assistant secretary of defense for special operations and low-intensity conflict, a coordinating board for low-intensity conflict within the National Security Council, and a new major force program, that is, a separate budgetary category for Special Operations Forces. The final bill, which became known as the Nunn-Cohen Amendment to the 1987 Defense Authorization Act, was signed into law in October 1986.[63]

The establishment of the command has done much to improve special operations, which in the 1970s and 1980s were characterized by a low state of readiness, ad hoc command and control, and lack of focus. U.S. Special Operations Forces are now second to none in quality. Several years ago, Special Operations Command was designated a supported command in the war on terrorism.

What makes the Special Operations Command problematic for civil-military relations, however, is the classified nature of much of what these forces do. Specifically, there is a problem of oversight. The United States has always had clandestine operators—for example, much of what the CIA does is classified—but these long-standing intelligence functions are subject to scrutiny by special congressional committees. Congress currently lacks the same sort of oversight regarding "direct action" by Special Operations Forces. As a result, there is no genuine civilian control of the command.

The Use of the Military in Domestic Affairs

One of the questions raised at the beginning of this essay concerns the appropriate mission of the military. We have already looked at the issue of a war-fighting vs. constabulary emphasis. But this question also raises the issue of whether the military should have a foreign or domestic focus.

Contrary to what many Americans believe, the Constitution itself does not prohibit the use of the military in domestic affairs. Indeed, the U.S. military has intervened in domestic affairs frequently since the founding of the Republic. In 1792, Congress passed two laws that permitted implementation of Congress's constitutional power "to provide for calling forth the militia to execute the laws of the union, suppress insurrections and repel invasions": the Militia Act and the "Calling Forth" Act, which gave the president limited authority to employ the militia in the event of domestic emergencies. In 1807, at the behest of President Thomas Jefferson, who was troubled by his inability to use the regular army as well as the militias to deal with the Burr conspiracy of 1806–7, Congress also declared the army to be an enforcer of federal laws, not only as a separate force, but as a part of the *posse comitatus* or local militia.[64]

In 1854, Franklin Pierce's attorney general, Caleb Cushing, issued an opinion that supported the congressional declaration, and troops were often used in the antebellum period to enforce the fugitive slave laws and suppress domestic violence between pro- and antislavery factions during the struggle in "Bloody Kansas." Soldiers and marines participated in the capture of John Brown at Harpers Ferry in 1859.

After the Civil War, the U.S. Army was involved in supporting the Reconstruction governments in the southern states, and it was the army's role in preventing the intimidation of black voters and Republicans at southern polling places that led to the passage of the Posse Comitatus Act. In the election of 1876, President Ulysses S. Grant deployed army units as a *posse comitatus* in support of federal marshals maintaining order at the polls. In that election, Rutherford B. Hayes defeated Samuel Tilden with the disputed electoral votes of South Carolina, Louisiana, and Florida. Southerners claimed that the army had been misused to "rig" the election.

While the Posse Comitatus Act is usually portrayed as the triumph of the Democratic Party in ending Reconstruction, it is instructive to recall that the army itself welcomed the legislation precisely because it limited military involvement in civil affairs. The use of soldiers as a posse removed them from their own chain of command and placed them in the uncomfortable position of taking orders from local authorities who had an interest in the disputes that provoked the unrest in the first place. As a result, many officers came to believe that the involvement of the army in domestic policing was corrupting the institution.

Events such as the 9/11 attacks and Hurricane Katrina, which overwhelmed local, state, and federal agencies, have led some to call for an expansion of the military's role in domestic affairs, including law enforcement. "The question raised by the Katrina fiasco," wrote Daniel Henninger of the *Wall Street Journal*, "is whether the threat from madmen and nature is now sufficiently huge in its potential horror and unacceptable loss that we should modify existing jurisdictional authority to give the Pentagon functional first-responder status."[65]

In the wake of Katrina, President Bush concluded that it was indeed time to rethink the military's role. In a national address in September of 2005, President Bush asked Congress to consider a larger role for U.S. armed forces in responding to natural disasters. In this new role the Defense Department would "become the lead agency in coordinating and leading the response effort" to a large-scale disaster. Bush implied that the military is suited to this role because it is "the institution of our government most capable of massive logistical operations on a moment's notice."[66]

Some in Congress agreed. Even before the president's speech, Republican senator John Warner, chairman of the Senate Armed Services Committee, wrote a letter to Defense Secretary Donald Rumsfeld saying that his committee would be looking into "the entire legal framework governing a President's power to use the regular armed forces to restore public order in . . . a large-scale, protracted emergency." He asked the secretary of defense to take the issue under consideration. In response, Secretary Rumsfeld informed Senator Warner that the Pentagon was reviewing pertinent laws, including the 1878 Posse Comitatus Act, to determine whether revisions that would give the military a greater role during major domestic disasters were needed.[67]

This interest in increasing the military's role in domestic affairs is certainly understandable. The military is capable of responding to a massive disaster in ways that local, state, and other federal agencies most often can't. But those who demand a greater domestic role for the military must consider the impact of such a step on healthy civil-military relations in the United States. In addition, they must also take account of the fear historically expressed by officers that involving the military in domestic tasks will undermine the war-fighting capabilities of their units and cause their "fighting spirit" to decline.

In a fictional account of America after a military coup, Charles Dunlap, an air force staff judge advocate officer (and now a major general), demonstrates that the massive diversion of military forces to civilian uses—the requirement that the military undertake new, nontraditional missions and escalate its commitment to formerly ancillary duties—is a potentially dangerous business.[68] Dunlap rightly suggests that the military's new responsibilities would incorporate it into the political process to an unprecedented degree and hence dangerously politicize it. Moreover, they would have the perverse effect of diverting focus and resources from the military's central mission of combat training and fighting.

The problems with this new military—one more involved in politics, less capable as a fighting force—would be exacerbated if Congress amended laws to permit increased military participation in domestic affairs. We need to remember that the main reason Congress passed the Posse Comitatus Act in 1878 was concern that the army was being politicized.

In fact the Posse Comitatus Act is widely misunderstood. It does not bar the use of the military in domestic affairs. It does, however, make sure that such use is authorized only by the highest constitutional authority: Congress and the president. And this is the crux of the issue. The Posse Comitatus Act prohibits the use of the military to aid civil authorities in enforcing the law or suppressing civil disturbances *except in cases and under circumstances expressly authorized by the Constitution or Act of Congress* (see Section 1385, Title 18 U.S.C.; italics added). As the foremost authority on the use of the military in domestic affairs has written:

> All that [the Posse Comitatus Act] really did *was to repeal a doctrine whose only substantial foundation was an opinion by an attorney general* [Caleb Cushing], *and one that had never been tested in the courts. The president's power to use both regulars and militia remained undisturbed by the Posse Comitatus Act.* . . . But the Posse Comitatus Act did mean that *troops could not be used on any lesser authority than that of the president* and he must issue a "cease and desist" proclamation before he did so. Commanders in the field

would no longer have any discretion but must wait for orders from Washington.[69]

Those who seek to expand the military's role in domestic affairs need to ask themselves if they really want to return to the days when a "lesser authority" than the president could use the military for domestic purposes. The issue here is the quality of American civil-military relations and the health of the military establishment, both of which would suffer if the armed forces took on a greater civil mission.

Civil-Military Tensions in the Obama Administration

Writing before the 2008 election, Richard Kohn predicted that "the new administration, like its predecessors, will wonder to what extent it can exercise civilian 'control.' If the historical pattern holds, the administration will do something clumsy or overreact, provoking even more distrust simply in the process of establishing its own authority."[70] As recent events have illustrated, he was right on the money.

Obama, perhaps inadvertently, sowed the seeds of the current civil-military discord with his campaign rhetoric, which used Afghanistan as a club to beat the Republicans in general and the party's presidential candidate, John McCain, in particular over the head about Iraq. In Obama's formulation, Afghanistan became the "good war" and "the central front on terror" from which we had been distracted by our misadventure in Iraq. Yet once he was elected and confronted with the political difficulty of this stance, he backpedaled.

In keeping with his promise to reinvigorate the effort in Afghanistan, President Obama announced in March a "comprehensive new strategy . . . to reverse the Taliban's gains and promote a more capable and accountable Afghan government," pledging to properly resource this "war of necessity."[71] The new operational strategy called for a counterinsurgency approach (like that of the surge in Iraq) and focused on the security of the population; it rejected the "counterterrorism" approach (which NATO had followed during the Bush years) that used special operations forces and air strikes launched from unmanned aircraft to hunt down and kill al Qaeda terrorists.

President Obama even replaced the U.S. commander in Afghanistan, General David McKiernan, with General Stanley McChrystal, who had been General Petraeus's right-hand man in Iraq when a counterinsurgency strategy was successfully implemented.

But when McChrystal indicated in a confidential study completed in August that more troops would be needed to pursue the president's strategy, President Obama did nothing. Admiral Michael Mullen, chairman of the joint chiefs, told Congress that more troops would be needed; and experts suggested that the number of additional soldiers and Marines necessary to execute the new strategy was thirty to forty thousand. But this was apparently a truth Obama did not want to hear. In contrast to George Bush in 2007, who pursued what he thought was the right approach in Iraq despite the unpopularity of his decision, President Obama apparently began to rethink his hard line in Afghanistan out of concern that his base did not support any troop increase.

The perception that the president's actions regarding Afghanistan were motivated by political factors rather than strategic ones—a perception that undermined healthy civil-military relations—was reinforced by several clumsy missteps by the administration. These included the naked attempt by retired Marine General James Jones, the national security adviser, to intimidate military commanders in Afghanistan into reducing their troop requests to a politically acceptable level, and a White House directive to the Pentagon not to forward a request for more troops.[72] The most serious mistake, reported in the *Wall Street Journal*, was that the White House ordered General McChrystal not to testify before Congress.[73] This move furthered the perception that the administration was trying to muzzle the military.

News reports indicate that officers on General McChrystal's staff and elsewhere are frustrated by the president's failure to make a decision about how to proceed in Afghanistan, and about perceived attempts to muzzle the general by cutting off his legitimate access to Congress. They wonder why, after having declared the conflict there a "war of necessity," the president has not provided the necessary means to fight it properly. They wonder why, having selected McChrystal to turn things around in Afghanistan, President Obama has not supported him the way that George Bush supported Petraeus in Iraq.[74]

It is easy to see the truth of Kohn's prediction that a clumsy step by the administration would sow distrust on the part of the soldiers, thereby increasing civil-military tensions, but the steps taken by some in the military have made the situation worse. First someone leaked General McChrystal's strategic assessment to Bob Woodward of the *Washington Post*. Then an article published by McClatchy quoted anonymous officers to the effect that McChrystal would resign if the president did not give him what he needed to implement the announced strategy.[75] Such actions on the part of the uniformed military are symptoms of a continuing civil-military relations problem: they reflect the widespread belief among military officers that they should be advocates of particular policies rather than simply serving in their traditional advisory role.

Conclusion

Since the end of the Cold War, the United States has been involved in a painful renegotiation of the civil-military bargain. There is no question that this renegotiation has been exacerbated by war and the imperative to transform the U.S. military in order to better fight that war and future wars. Maintaining balanced civil-military relations is difficult in the best of times, and harder still during a period of war and transformation, both of which are inherently disruptive. It is no surprise that civil-military tensions increase during wartime. Nevertheless, reducing these tensions should remain an enduring goal of both civil and military leaders.

Right now the American people hold the U.S. military in high esteem. But the public animosity that has characterized the civil-military nexus since 9/11 (e.g., the "revolt of the generals") may well cause Americans to lose confidence and trust in the military. The high regard for the U.S. military may decline if the public comes to view the military as just another special interest group vying for more resources as it seeks to restrict how the civilian authorities use the military instrument,[76] or if retired soldiers are perceived to be no different from the political appointees who, having just left the administration, go on to peddle tell-all books intended to settle scores with adversaries.[77]

Finally, our admiration for the soldier, no matter how experienced in military affairs he may be, is still based on his conduct of operations and military strategy. It is up to the *statesman* to take the broader view, deciding when political considerations take precedence over even the most pressing military matters. The soldier must remain an adviser, not a policymaker.

3

Centralization vs. Decentralization: Preparing for and Practicing Mission Command in Counterinsurgency Operations

H. R. McMaster

Neither the numerous organizational changes that have taken place since 500 B.C., nor the technical advances that were introduced after about 1850, have significantly altered or even reduced the quintessential problem facing any command system, that of dealing with uncertainty. Though such advances, from the semaphore to the observation balloon, have often misled contemporaries into thinking the problem would be solved or at least diminished, in the end those hopes were invariably disappointed.[1]

—MARTIN VAN CREVELD, *Command in War*

In Afghanistan and Iraq, the United States and its coalition partners are engaged in missions that many believers in the "revolution in military affairs" and "defense transformation" failed to consider in the 1990s: protracted counterinsurgency and state-building efforts that require population security, security- sector reform, reconstruction and economic development, development of governmental capacity, and the establishment of rule of law. Counterinsurgency operations in Afghanistan and Iraq have demonstrated that, despite the many benefits of new communications, information, and surveillance technologies, war remains firmly in the realm of uncertainty. The complexity and uniqueness of local conditions confound efforts to generalize about all areas in which counterinsurgent forces are operating. Before September 11, many in the U.S. military and defense communities advocated concepts such as "rapid decisive operations" and "effects-based operations"; these concepts evoked images of commanders and staffs directing precise strikes from high-technology command posts to "achieve effects." Recent and ongoing military experiences, however, highlight the need to decentralize command. Higher-level commanders must be comfortable with relinquishing control and authority to junior commanders while setting conditions for effective decentralized operations consistent with the U.S. Army's concept of mission command.

This essay is an attempt to apply what practical combat experience has taught us to a persistent doctrinal debate within the U.S. military. The conclusion is that complex forms of what some have labeled "irregular warfare"—conflicts in which the political rather than technological dynamics determine the outcome—will require America's fighting men and women to devolve decision making downward and forward. But to paraphrase Clausewitz, what seems simple in war is often very difficult. Effective decentralization of command does not just happen. Senior commanders have to prepare their organizations and leaders for decentralized operations and develop a common approach to integrating decentralized operations that contributes to the achievement of policy goals and objectives. Recent experience has been instructive in that connection and highlights the importance of continuities in command in war and, in particular, the concept of mission command.

Theory vs. the Reality of Counterinsurgency Warfare

U.S. Army doctrine for command and control in combat is grounded in the concept of mission command, defined as

> the conduct of military operations through decentralized execution based upon mission orders for effective mission accomplishment. Successful mission command results from subordinate leaders at all echelons exercising disciplined initiative within

the commander's intent to accomplish missions. It requires an environment of trust and mutual understanding.[2]

By the time of the 9/11 attacks, however, we had begun to stray from the concept of mission command. In the 1990s, the belief that advances in military technology had revolutionized the conduct of war inspired a trend toward centralizing the command and control of military forces. Some assumed that communication, computer, and information technologies would allow the military to create a "collaborative information environment" and use a process called "operational net assessment" to gain a high degree of understanding of the environment and the enemy. Commanders and staffs remote from an area of operation would acquire "dominant battlespace knowledge" upon which they would base the development of near-perfect plans and precise orders. Because it was assumed that these technologies would "lift the fog of war," strategy was largely reduced to a targeting exercise that aimed to destroy critical "nodes" in an enemy "system."[3]

The U.S. Joint Forces Command Futures Lab developed concepts that emphasized centralized planning, the careful synchronization of discrete operations and actions, and efficiency in the application of military force. The concept of effects-based operations, for example, speculated that the enemy could be fully understood through operational net assessment, a method that was thought to provide "a comprehensive system-of-systems understanding of the enemy and the environment" and reveal even second- and third-order effects. Thus U.S. forces would progress linearly and rapidly toward victory. The enemy organization would be unable to respond effectively as it fell victim to "cumulative and cascading effects."[4] Staffs would be able to calculate precisely the specific military actions and the level of effort necessary to achieve desired effects. The application of force, therefore, could be very efficient and subject to a high degree of control.

These concepts influenced thinking about command in war, which, it seemed, was being subsumed within processes like operational net assessment and effects-based operations. Constructive simulations designed to validate these processes masked flawed assumptions concerning the degree of situational understanding that technology could deliver and, in turn, reinforced the belief that future war would be quantifiable, predictable, short in duration, and efficient. This approach to war disconnected military operations from policy goals and objectives as well as the human, psychological, and cultural dimensions of conflict. The use of PowerPoint to develop and present plans exacerbated this problem. Sentence fragments used as bullet points obscured flaws and disconnects in logic and coherence, while colorful charts and complicated graphics created an illusion of authoritativeness.

Advocates of concepts like dominant battlespace knowledge, operational net assessment, and network-centric operations assumed that technologies that permitted U.S. air and naval forces to dominate the aerospace and sea domains would have a similar effect when applied on land. They ignored the factors that increase the complexity and uncertainty of land warfare— geography, culture, the interaction with an adaptive land-based enemy, and the requirement to use other instruments of power along with force to achieve political objectives. Even the U.S. Army seemed to accept uncritically the assertion that technology would permit a high degree of situational understanding that would, in turn, allow the efficient application of force to achieve rapid and decisive results. The 2001 edition of the Army's capstone doctrinal manual asserted that soldiers and units would have near-perfect intelligence:

> Unmanned systems with artificial intelligence will augment human action and decision making through improved situational understanding. . . . The extensive information available to Army leaders will also allow unprecedented awareness of every aspect of future operations. Precise knowledge of the enemy and friendly situations will facilitate exact tailoring of units for mission requirements; tactical employment of precision fires; exploitative, decisive maneuver at extended ranges; and responsive, flexible support of those forces. . . . Improved command and control systems will enable leaders to know far more than ever before about the nature of activities in their battlespace. They will have access to highly accurate information regarding enemy and friendly locations, the civil population, terrain, and weather. . . . The common operational picture provided through integration of real-time intelligence and accurate targeting reduces the need to fill space with forces and direct-fire weapons. Agile forces can also improve the capacity of commanders to employ combat

power with precision to achieve a desired outcome. The goal of future Army operations will be to simultaneously attack critical targets throughout the area of operations by rapid maneuver and precision fires to break the adversary's will and compel him to surrender. The cumulative effect of simultaneous shaping operations and nearly simultaneous decisive operations will be to reduce an adversary's ability to synchronize his effort and will establish the military conditions for friendly victory— decisive victory.[5]

An emphasis on control and applying combat power with precision seemed to be eclipsing the Army concept of mission command. An omniscient headquarters would allocate precisely the resources a subordinate commander needed, target the enemy, and deliver victory quickly, cheaply, and efficiently.

Even after it became clear that, contrary to prewar assumptions, achieving coalition objectives in Afghanistan and Iraq required sustained counterinsurgency campaigns and state-building efforts, thinking associated with concepts like rapid decisive operations and effects-based operations led some military leaders to adopt a raiding approach to counterinsurgency. This approach used technical-intelligence collection to direct raids against critical "nodes" in an insurgent network. The idea was that killing or capturing key insurgent leaders and facilitators would disrupt the enemy and allow indigenous forces to gain strength and eventually take the lead in counterinsurgency efforts. This approach elevated one important capability in counterinsurgency to the level of strategy. It did not adequately address fundamental causes of violence, critical sources of enemy strength, the enemy strategy, likely enemy reactions, or the effect of actions on the population. Brutal and determined enemies, the weakness of the Afghan and Iraqi states, and the constantly shifting character of the conflicts in those countries led to the abandonment of the raiding approach, which had its roots in the flawed prewar visions of future conflict.

As U.S. forces adapted to the demands of counterinsurgency, they shifted toward population security and a comprehensive counterinsurgency approach. The population-centric approach required a high degree of decentralization, additional forces, and more time. Innovation and adaptation in Iraq and Afghanistan would not be delivered by a system of systems process; rather, they required the "environment of trust and mutual understanding" called for in the Army's concept of mission command.

Counterinsurgency Demands Decentralization

That forces must secure the population while working closely with indigenous military, police, and civil officials is the fundamental reason why effective counterinsurgency operations must be decentralized. In contrast to the large-scale targeting exercises that defense transformation advocates envisioned, counterinsurgency operations at the tactical level are conducted on two principal battlegrounds, those of intelligence and of perception.[6]

To collect the human intelligence necessary to identify an enemy that hides among the population and intimidates people to retain anonymity and freedom of movement, the counterinsurgent force must lift the pall of fear off the populace through effective security operations. If forces operate in a centralized manner from large bases, the insurgent force will retain the initiative and control the population. Under constant threat from insurgents, people will avoid interaction with counterinsurgent forces and refuse to offer information.

Decentralization is also essential to winning on the battleground of perception. Counterinsurgent forces must be present to counter enemy propaganda and disinformation. If forces rely principally on a raiding approach to counterinsurgency, the only counterinsurgent actions visible to the population will tend to reinforce rather than counter enemy propaganda that portrays counterinsurgent forces as oppressive and predatory. Winning on the battleground of perception requires maximizing positive contact with the population and countering enemy propaganda with deeds and actions. It also requires discrimination in the use of firepower to protect innocents. Raids or precision strikes against insurgent networks are an important component of a comprehensive counterinsurgency approach, but if these tactics are applied without securing the population, they risk doing more harm than good. Deeds and actions—building relationships and addressing local grievances—are the best means to clarify counterinsurgent intentions, counter enemy propaganda, and bolster the legitimacy of the government and the security forces. Such a comprehensive effort requires forces to be there, living among the population.

Moreover, physical decentralization alone is insufficient. Junior leaders must also have the authority to make decisions and act. Whenever possible, local commanders should control the resources necessary to secure the population and defeat the enemy in their area. U.S. Army and Marine Corps counterinsurgency (COIN) doctrine, published in December 2006, acknowledges the requirement for decentralizing authority and capabilities:

> Mission command is ideally suited to the mosaic nature of COIN operations. Local commanders have the best grasp of their situations. Under mission command, they are given access to or control of the resources needed to produce timely intelligence, conduct effective tactical operations, and manage [information operations] and civil-military operations. Thus, effective COIN operations are decentralized, and higher commanders owe it to their subordinates to push as many capabilities as possible down to their level. Mission command encourages the initiative of subordinates and facilitates the learning that must occur at every level. It is a major characteristic of a COIN force that can adapt and react as least as quickly as the insurgents.[7]

Physical decentralization permits junior leaders to understand and cope with the complexity of the situation. The decentralization of authority and resources allows military units to act quickly and adapt to the evolving nature of the conflict at the local level.

Decentralization, however, is sometimes resisted because centralization is considered more efficient, especially in allocating resources in high demand, such as human intelligence teams or aerial surveillance assets. To apply air and space resources most efficiently, for example, U.S. Air Force doctrine calls for control "by a single airman who maintains the broad, strategic perspective necessary to balance and prioritize the use of a powerful, highly desired yet limited force. A single air commander, focused on the broader aspects of an operation, can best mediate the competing demands for tactical support against the strategic and operational requirements of the conflict."[8]

The Air Force's preference for centralized control is in tension with the army's concept of mission command. That tension is evident in views of how to allocate and control intelligence, surveillance, and reconnaissance (ISR) assets. In an article written with two members of his staff, Army general Raymond Odierno, the commander of Multinational Force–Iraq, made the case for decentralization, arguing that "the effective use of ISR is enabled through decentralized control that provides the greatest amount of flexibility at the lowest levels of command." He urged that "on a decentralized battlefield, commanders charged with responsibilities to achieve successful outcomes to complex problems should be given all available means to enable success."[9]

The need to decentralize command and control in Iraq and Afghanistan has led some to describe these conflicts as "colonels' wars." Philip Zelikow, long an observer and practitioner of strategy-making at the highest levels of the American government and former special counselor to Secretary of State Condoleeza Rice, observes that the conflict in Iraq "is a colonel's war or major's war; it's battalion-level, and maybe even below. It's a highly local form of conflict in which everything needs to be adapted to local circumstances and informed by local information." However, if units are unprepared or if they receive inadequate direction, decentralization can result in inconsistent and even contradictory efforts. Effective counterinsurgency operations demand coordination between levels of command to connect efforts at the local, provincial, and national levels, as Zelikow notes:

> You have to have a strategy countrywide that tells your battalion and company commanders what their jobs are. They then have to have a lot of autonomy for the execution of those jobs and the execution of that strategy adapted to local circumstances. But they have to be trained in an approach to the problem.[10]

Counterinsurgency operations demand decentralization but also require a common understanding of the nature of the conflict, clearly articulated objectives, a comprehensive operational plan, and close coordination between levels of command, civil authorities, indigenous leaders, and adjacent organizations. It is critical for senior leaders to prepare small units and junior leaders for the considerable challenges of protracted counterinsurgency campaigns. Particular attention must be paid to the training and education of junior officers and noncommissioned officers, who must develop a high degree of competence in combat and civil-military skills, understand the environment in which they will operate, and lead their soldiers aggressively while maintaining the highest moral and ethical standards. The next section outlines the training and education that soldiers and leaders require.

Preparation for Decentralized Counterinsurgency Operations

Properly trained soldiers and officers are not only able to defeat the enemy in battle; they are also more likely to win the war of perception. If counterinsurgents demonstrate determination and competence, they will begin to tip the scales of popular perception against the insurgent organization. The population must believe that the counterinsurgent force will win before they will risk cooperation with or participate in the effort to defeat the insurgency and establish enduring security.[11]

The best-trained soldiers fighting against an insurgency receive training or education in five areas: combat; civil-military tasks; culture and history; ethics; and stress management.

Combat. Training for decentralized operations in a counterinsurgency environment must aim to develop a high level of combat skill. Soldiers must be able to operate all of their weapons with speed and accuracy under all conditions. They must be trained to fight in small units that can operate in and among the population; their goal is to defeat insurgent organizations while minimizing the threat to innocents. (Toward that end, units should have as many snipers and marksmen as possible. Armored vehicles and the mobile protected firepower they bring to the fight permit units to move through contested areas, provide responsive support to dismounted forces, and overwhelm the enemy with discriminate, precision direct fire. Units should also integrate engineering, logistical, and maintenance capabilities for mobility support and protection.) Because small, widely dispersed units may not have a medic with them at all times, all soldiers should receive advanced first aid training; medical support must be responsive and located as far forward as possible. Units must become expert in conducting reconnaissance and security operations, as these are the tactical missions that permit the force to protect the population, guard against surprise, develop the intelligence necessary to pursue the enemy, and dictate the terms of battle.[12]

Leaders in counterinsurgency operations must be proficient in the same skills that are required in major combat operations: they must be able to integrate fire and maneuver, integrate air and ground operations, plan direct fire, coordinate with flank units, fight and report simultaneously, and issue clear, succinct orders. It is vital that junior leaders know how to integrate the broad range of combined-arms and joint capabilities such as combat engineering and close air support. Specialized capabilities such as psychological operations teams, civil affairs teams, and interpreters are also critical to small-unit success.

The confidence that comes with proper training is critical to the development of combat prowess. Confidence serves as a bulwark against fear, which can paralyze units or lead to the disintegration of combat teams. To build confidence, training must replicate the conditions of combat as closely as possible. Training exercises must capture the uncertainty of combat by injecting change, rushed timelines, casualties, and bad information into all exercises.

Uncertainty is one of the principal causes of combat stress, and stress has a corrosive effect on soldiers and units over time, slowly but inexorably reducing their effectiveness.[13] But realistic training under uncertain conditions can build soldiers' confidence, help protect them from the debilitating effects of a dangerous counterinsurgency environment, and enable them to act quickly enough to defeat an enemy who seeks to fight only when he has the benefit of surprise.

Civil-military tasks. But developing combat skills and building confident and capable combined-arms teams constitute only the "price of admission" to counterinsurgency operations.[14] As David Galula observed in his classic book, *Counterinsurgency Warfare: Theory and Practice*, "tasks and responsibilities cannot be neatly divided between the civilian and the soldier, for their operations overlap too much with each other."[15] Civil-military operations— such as efforts to conduct reconstruction, establish basic services, strengthen governance and rule of law, and develop police forces—must be fully integrated into the counterinsurgency effort. Otherwise, the weakness of the state and grievances associated with the government's inability to satisfy the basic needs of the population create opportunities for the insurgent and undermine improvements in security.

If civilian officials are not available to undertake critical state-building tasks, soldiers and military officers must be prepared to fill that gap. Political and economic initiatives from the top are likely to fail unless there is follow-through at the local level. Where there is a lack of civilian resources or a dangerous security environment, military forces will have to connect the development effort to the local level. Galula argued that

> to confine soldiers to purely military functions while urgent and vital tasks have to be done and nobody else is available to undertake them, would be senseless. The soldier must then be prepared to become a propagandist, a social worker, a civil engineer, a schoolteacher, a nurse, a boy scout.[16]

The Army counterinsurgency manual is consistent with this view:

> The more extensive the U.S. participation is in a COIN and the more dispersed U.S. forces are throughout a country, the greater the need for additional mechanisms to extend civilian oversight and assistance. However, given the limited resources of the Department of State and the other U.S. Government agencies, military forces often represent the country team in decentralized and diffuse operational environments. Operating with a clear understanding of the guiding political aims, members of the military at all levels must be prepared to exercise judgment and act without the benefit of immediate civilian oversight and control.[17]

Senior leaders must help prepare junior leaders for the broad range of responsibilities associated with civil-military operations. Preparation should draw on developmental expertise and international best practices, but mainly emphasize learning indigenous systems and identifying how soldiers might help make those systems work.

Culture and history. Soldiers must also develop an understanding of the history and culture of the region in which they are fighting and must be familiar with the ethnic, tribal, and sectarian dynamics at the local level. Thus some units send selected soldiers to undergraduate history, anthropology, or regional studies courses as well as to language training.[18] Although soldiers and leaders harbor no illusions that these courses will develop expert knowledge or a high degree of language competency, they believe they will prepare soldiers to interact positively with and ask the right questions of the indigenous population. Understanding the culture and history of the region allows soldiers and leaders to anticipate and consider likely second- and third-order effects of their actions, as well as to evaluate sources of information—especially important in an insurgency, where all sides seek to influence counterinsurgent forces through disinformation.[19] A basic level of cultural and historical understanding allows soldiers to listen to a broad range of people, consider the sources of information, and begin to develop a holistic understanding of the situation. Soldiers familiar with the history and culture of the region in which they are operating tend to experience less stress from being in an unfamiliar setting and are thus better able to cope with the stresses of combat.

It is useful for soldiers to study history because, as they become familiar with previous counterinsurgency experiences, they gain a valuable comparative perspective. Knowledge of history also fosters moral conduct in counterinsurgency operations by generating empathy for the population. If soldiers understand the population's situation, their feelings of confusion and frustration might be supplanted with concern and compassion. A soldier who knows what the Iraqi people have gone through, for instance— three decades of brutal dictatorship, a destructive eight-year war with Iran, and the sanctions regime after the 1991 Gulf War—is more likely to see the population's passivity as a survival mechanism and not reflective of true support for the enemy. Indeed, the U.S. counterinsurgency manual describes "genuine compassion and empathy for the populace" as an "effective weapon against insurgents."[20]

Because insurgents often depend on sponsorship from an aggrieved community, and because junior leaders conducting security operations can find themselves thrust into the role of mediators, soldiers' education in language, culture, and history should be supplemented with education and training in negotiation and conflict resolution. Understanding the interests, fears, aspirations, and grievances of various communities is necessary for mediating between factions and encouraging them to resolve differences politically rather than violently. For this reason, training that involves role playing, especially with expatriates from the relevant communities, helps leaders develop the skills, understanding, and confidence they will need to mediate effectively. Counterinsurgent leaders should attempt to build toward direct dialogue among the parties in conflict and help strengthen or develop mediating mechanisms that indigenous leaders can sustain in the long term.[21]

While it is important that all soldiers possess a basic grasp of the culture and history of the area in which they are fighting, it is also important that leaders and units have access to expertise in these areas even as they operate dispersed over wide areas. Particularly valuable are historical studies of the subregion in which a unit is operating, especially succinct histories of districts and provinces that cover the causes and conduct of previous armed conflicts. To meet this need, the U.S. military established its Human Terrain Team program, which pairs cultural anthropologists and area specialists with deployed combat brigades. These experts as well as trusted indigenous leaders help deepen soldiers' understanding of the tribal, ethnic, and sectarian dynamics in an area and show how those dynamics influence and are connected to the broader counterinsurgency effort. While some systems analysts have argued that holistic understanding can be delivered through "reachback" to databases, soldiers will find that there is no substitute for working with an expert in close contact with local conditions and the population. Academic experts understand the larger cultural dynamics, but without in-depth knowledge of the local situation, their advice is of limited utility to leaders at the platoon and company levels.

Ethics. Decentralized counterinsurgency requires discipline and the maintenance of moral and ethical standards of conduct. The counterinsurgency manual directs leaders to "work proactively to establish and maintain the proper ethical climate of their organizations" and "ensure that the trying counterinsurgency environment does not undermine the values of their Soldiers and Marines." Soldiers and Marines "must remain faithful to basic American, Army, and Marine Corps standards of proper behavior and respect for the sanctity of life."[22] Indiscriminate force or abuse of prisoners or the population not only causes the obvious harm to its victims, but can have a devastating effect on the mission and the psychological well-being of a military organization.

The counterinsurgency manual recognizes that ensuring moral conduct during counterinsurgency operations is particularly difficult because "the environment that fosters insurgency is characterized by violence, immorality, distrust, and deceit."[23] Moreover, the standard of success for the insurgent is very low; the insurgent organization's immediate aim might be only to incite fear and chaos, erode faith in the government's ability to fulfill its principal responsibilities, and increase popular discontent. Whereas the insurgent might seek to tear society apart and pit various communities against one another as a means of destroying an old order or preventing the establishment of a new one, the counterinsurgent must reestablish security, rekindle hope, allay fears, and help convince communities that their aspirations can be realized through peaceful means. Provoking a heavy-handed or indiscriminate response from the counterinsurgent is an often-used insurgent and terrorist tactic. As the U.S. counterinsurgency manual observes:

> One of the insurgents' most effective ways to undermine and erode political will is to portray their opposition as untrustworthy or illegitimate. These attacks work especially well when insurgents can portray their opposition as unethical by the opposition's own standards. To combat these efforts, Soldiers and Marines treat noncombatants and detainees humanely, according to American values and internationally recognized human rights standards. In COIN, preserving noncombatant lives and dignity is central to mission accomplishment.[24]

Decentralized operations place a great deal of responsibility on the shoulders of junior leaders for ensuring moral conduct. It is junior officers and noncommissioned officers who will enforce standards and make critical time-sensitive decisions under pressure.

Senior commanders, however, play a critical role in establishing the proper ethical climate as well as preparing junior leaders and soldiers to maintain moral and ethical standards despite the difficult environment and the unscrupulousness of the enemy. Leaders must balance the need to condition soldiers and units to overcome fear and to fight the enemy with the need to inoculate them against abuses and excesses. Achieving that balance requires psychological as well as ethical preparation. Methods include applied ethics education; training that replicates difficult situations that soldiers are likely to encounter; education about the cultures and historical experiences of the peoples among whom the wars are being fought; and leadership that strives to set the example, keep soldiers informed, and manage combat stress.

As Christopher Coker observes in *The Warrior Ethos*, individual and institutional values are more important than legal constraints on immoral behavior. Legal contracts are often observed only as long as others honor them or as long as they are enforced.[25] U.S. Army and Marine Corps applied-ethics education aims, in part, to inform soldiers and marines about the covenant between them, their institutions, and society.[26] The collective nature of ethics training is immensely important; soldiers should conduct training as units and understand that the institution and their fellow soldiers expect them to exhibit a higher sense of honor than that to which they are exposed in the culture at large. Particularly important is the soldier's recognition that he or she is expected to take risks and make sacrifices to accomplish the mission, protect fellow soldiers or safeguard innocents. Use of force that reduces risk to the soldier but places either the mission or innocents at risk must be seen as inconsistent with the military's code of honor and professional ethics.[27]

While leaders emphasize ethical behavior as an end, commanders should also underscore the utilitarian basis for sustaining high moral and professional standards. Showing soldiers how the enemy portrays them in propaganda videos—and pointing out how soldiers' behavior can either strengthen or counter that propaganda—is a particularly effective means of communicating that moral transgressions can strengthen the enemy, place the mission in jeopardy, and bring discredit upon themselves and their fellow soldiers.

Stress management. But applied ethics education alone is insufficient to preserve moral character under the intense emotional and psychological pressures of combat. U.S. military leaders understand that managing stress is critical to preserving the humaneness of their soldiers as they confront arduous conditions.[28] Combat trauma is often a major cause of unprofessional or immoral behavior. Soldiers and leaders must be prepared to endure intense psychological and emotional pressures. In decentralized operations, routine access to mental health professionals is problematic. Officers and sergeants must understand their responsibility to help soldiers manage combat stress. They should learn about critical topics such as grief work, critical-event debriefing, and the warning signs of combat trauma.[29] Because stress is the most difficult dimension of combat to replicate in training, leaders ought to be encouraged to read, think, and talk about their responsibilities in this area.[30] Senior leaders must continuously emphasize that commitment to fellow troopers and the mission must be the motivating factor in battle—not rage. Leaders should also ensure that the expression of grief is not stigmatized, and help "communalize" grief so soldiers can get through difficult times together.

Ensuring the psychological well-being critical to preserving discipline and moral conduct in combat depends in large measure on preserving soldiers' sense of agency or control. The best way to protect soldiers against the frustration and anger that can erode a unit's professionalism is success in counterinsurgency operations, achieved through securing the population and making it impossible for the enemy to hide in plain sight. Once the insurgent can no longer intimidate, coerce, or count on support from the population, intelligence allows forces to gain the initiative and target the enemy precisely. Success in counterinsurgency operations also permits soldiers to see how their efforts have improved peoples' lives. Positive feedback reinforces ethical and moral conduct. Senior leaders must help soldiers understand how the risks they take and the sacrifices they make contribute to objectives worthy of those risks and sacrifices.[31] Success in operations combined with the knowledge that they have behaved morally helps soldiers avoid combat-related stress.

The Foundation for Operational Planning

While decentralization is an essential feature of effective counterinsurgency operations, lower-level tactics must be part of a well-designed operational plan and a fundamentally sound strategy. As Kimberly Kagan has observed, the problem of counterinsurgency is "not only localized, but also systemic."[32] Junior leaders and soldiers must understand how their actions fit into the overall plan to defeat the enemy and accomplish the mission. If they fail to address the systemic dimension of counterinsurgency, they limit counter-insurgent efforts and create opportunities for the insurgent organization.[33]

It is the job of the operational commander to coordinate these and other elements of the counterinsurgency campaign—to visualize, describe, and direct a comprehensive approach to defeating insurgents. Commanders at the operational level—that is, the level of war that "links the tactical employment of forces to national and military and strategic objectives" through the integration of "ends, conditions, ways, and means"—must prioritize and integrate efforts to achieve clearly defined goals and objectives.[34] Clear operational objectives and plans help ensure that the full range of activities and programs is consistent with and contributes to the achievement of policy goals. Sound operational plans are also essential to ensure consistency of effort among units, between military organizations and civil–military teams, and over time as the mission progresses.

In addition to integrating the efforts of subordinate organizations, operational commanders and senior civilian officials must help ensure consistency of effort within multinational coalitions and the interdepartmental civilian-military team. While it is helpful for departments in Washington to work together, it is vital that representatives of those departments at the operational level act as an integrated team. A campaign plan that is understood and accepted by all members of the multinational, civil-military team is the foundation for achieving unity of effort. The counter-insurgency manual emphasizes the importance of integrated civil-military operational design:

> Through [campaign] design commanders gain an understanding of the problem and the COIN operation's purpose within the strategic context. Communicating this understanding of the problem, purpose, and context to subordinates allows them to exercise subordinates' initiative. . . . Traditional aspects of campaign design . . . are not adequate for a discussion of the broader design construct for a COIN environment. . . . Military capabilities provide only one component of an overall

approach to a COIN campaign. Design of a COIN campaign must be viewed holistically. Only a comprehensive approach employing all relevant design components, including the other instruments of national power, is likely to reach the desired end state.[35]

The commander and the senior civilian official must form joint civil-military planning teams. Planners must have relevant expertise, knowledge of the situation, and the seniority and authority to speak for their departments.[36] When possible, planning teams should include representatives from the supported government and its security forces. If political sensitivities preclude their participation, it will be essential to consult these leaders widely to ensure that the operational plan works in concert with efforts of the supported government. But operational design itself begins with policy goals and objectives. Working backwards from these, the commander and the senior civilian official derive their mission and define what is to be achieved. The more clearly operational plans are connected to the accomplishment of policy goals (which themselves are derived from vital national interests), the more likely it is that sufficient resources will be available to accomplish the mission.

Equipped with an understanding of what is to be achieved, the commander and senior civilian official should use their planning team to help them understand the nature of the conflict. They must ask the big questions to ensure that plans and efforts are feasible and appropriate. As the eighteenth-century Prussian philosopher of war Carl von Clausewitz observed:

> The first, the supreme, the most far-reaching act of judgment that the statesman and commander have to make is to establish the kind of war on which they are embarking, neither mistaking it for, nor trying to turn it into, something that is alien to its nature. This is the first of all strategic questions and the most comprehensive.[37]

Planners need to identify and describe the causes of violence—which might include grievances that fuel an insurgency, actions of malign external actors (e.g., hostile states or transnational terrorist organizations), the weakness of the state, or communal competition for power and resources—because a plan that misunderstands the fundamental nature of the conflict is almost certain to fail. If operational design is not consistent with policy or the causes of violence, planning is likely to be driven by what planners might like to do, such as minimize the number of forces committed, avoid difficult state-building tasks, or transition rapidly to indigenous forces that are unprepared to assume full responsibility for security and critical government functions.

Because of the complexity and inherent uncertainty of counterinsurgency operations, all planning will be based on assumptions. Planners at the operational level must make those assumptions explicit and ensure that they are logical, essential to the plan, and realistic. If assumptions critical to the success of the plan are unrealistic, the plan will not be worth the paper on which it is written. As the conflict continues to evolve, commanders and their staffs must reexamine initial assumptions and adjust the plan if events or conditions invalidate them.

Effective planning, along with efforts at the operational level to carry out the plan and achieve policy goals, relies on accurate, comprehensive, and up-to-date intelligence. Intelligence efforts at the operational level must place the military situation in the context of the political, social, and economic dynamics that are shaping the course of events. In contrast to the assumption of "dominant battlespace knowledge" touted in the 1990s, the vast majority of intelligence in counterinsurgency comes from below and from human, rather than technical, sources. "Operational net assessment" and the "system of systems" understanding it is meant to provide are useful mainly for targeting the enemy. Intelligence that is placed in a political, social, or cultural context and subject to expert analysis, however, helps planners understand the dynamics that are most critical in shaping the outcome of the conflict. Whenever possible, those charged with developing plans at the operational level should travel to subordinate units and subregions within the country to gain a detailed understanding of the enemy and political, economic, and social dynamics at the local level. Visits should include meetings with local government officials, tribal or community leaders, and security force leaders. Planning teams must include military and civilian officials with deep historical and cultural knowledge of the country and the region.

Once they have developed the mission and objectives and have formed a comprehensive estimate, operational planners assist the commander and the senior civilian official in articulating the operational logic that will underpin the effort. The operational logic has two parts, a statement of the "commander's intent" and a statement of the "concept of operations." The intent describes the broad purpose of operations and key objectives that must be accomplished to ensure mission success. The overall concept of operations may be the most important part of an operational plan because it describes to military and civilian leaders how they will combine their own efforts as well as coordinate those efforts with the indigenous government and security forces to accomplish the mission.[38] The concept describes how the operational commander and senior civilian official see the effort developing over time based on the actions and programs they initiate, as well as the anticipated interaction of their plans with the enemy and other sources of instability. A sound concept is essential for allowing subordinate units and civil-military teams to take initiative. Conversely, a subordinate leader will be reluctant to take risks if there is uncertainty about the concept of operations. Moreover, a commonly understood concept serves as a foundation on which planners can develop detailed plans in critical focus areas or along what the military calls "logical lines of effort," for example the information or communications lines of effort that are so critical in counterinsurgency operations, while ensuring that those plans are consistent with the overall concept and are mutually reinforcing.

The Essential Elements of Operational Plans

Because counterinsurgency is fundamentally a political problem, the foundation for detailed planning must be a political strategy that drives all other initiatives, actions, and programs. David Galula observed that in counterinsurgency operations,

> politics becomes an active instrument of operation. And so intricate is the interplay between the political and the military actions that they cannot be tidily separated; on the contrary, every military move has to be weighed with regard to its political effects and vice versa.[39]

The general objective of the political strategy is to remove or reduce significantly the political basis for violence. The strategy must be consistent with the nature of the conflict and is likely to address fears, grievances, and interests that motivate active or tacit support for insurgents. Ultimately, the political strategy must endeavor to convince leaders of reconcilable armed groups that they can best protect and advance their interests through political participation rather than violence.

The political strategy must also foster and maintain a high degree of unity of effort between the supported government and the foreign forces and civil authorities supporting them. Unity of effort should be grounded in a common understanding of the nature of the conflict and agreement on the broad strategy necessary to defeat insurgent organizations and achieve sustainable security. If the indigenous government and its security forces act to exacerbate rather than ameliorate the causes of violence, the political strategy must address how best to demonstrate that an alternative approach is necessary to avert defeat and achieve an outcome consistent with the indigenous government's interests. If institutions or functions of the supported state are captured by malign or corrupt organizations that pursue agendas inconsistent with the political strategy, it may become necessary to employ a range of cooperative, persuasive, and coercive means to change that behavior and restore a cooperative relationship.

The military component of operational plans must support the political strategy by attacking the will and capabilities of insurgent groups and securing the population such that political development can proceed. Military forces relentlessly pursue "irreconcilables" not only to defeat the most committed and dangerous enemy organizations, but also to convince "reconcilables" to commit to political resolution of the conflict. As mentioned previously, defeating the insurgent's campaign of intimidation and coercion through effective population security operations is a necessary precondition for achieving political progress as well as for gaining the intelligence necessary to conduct effective offensive operations. The concept for military operations must be grounded in the intelligence estimate. Planners must understand the nature and structure of enemy organizations, their ideological or political philosophy, the strategy that they are pursuing, their sources of strength, and their vulnerabilities. Operations should aim to isolate enemy organizations from sources of strength while attacking enemy vulnerabilities in the physical, political, informational, and psychological domains.

Operational plans must integrate reform of the indigenous government's security agencies and the development of capable and legitimate security forces into the overall security effort in a way that is consistent with the political strategy. Unless the population trusts its own government and security forces to fulfill its most basic need—security—it will not be possible to defeat an insurgency or end a communal struggle associated with an insurgency. Local military units and civil-military teams focus on training and on operating alongside indigenous police and army units, while senior commanders, civilian officials, and their staffs focus on building the administrative capacity and professionalism of security ministries. Senior commanders must work with the host government to craft a plan for developing ministerial capacity that is grounded in a common understanding of security force roles and missions, and of the force structure necessary to fulfill them. Senior commanders must take a long view in that connection; plans must initiate work on systems and capabilities that take time to mature, such as leader development, financial management, personnel management, logistics, and infrastructure. Because indigenous forces will ultimately be responsible for maintaining security, security force capability must be great enough to maintain security after foreign supporting forces depart.

It is difficult to overstate the importance of identifying and developing capable leaders who are committed to improving the security of all citizens rather than advancing a particularistic agenda or their personal interests. Because the population's lack of trust and confidence in their security forces is often a grievance that fuels an insurgency, particular attention must be paid to the loyalty and professionalism of these forces (e.g., responsible leaders must be selected and recruits thoroughly screened), and there must be a sustained effort to introduce these forces to their own populations and build popular confidence in them. Because all insurgencies possess a dimension of civil conflict, it is important that operational planning for security-sector reform be wholly consistent with and reinforce the political strategy, that security forces be generally representative of the population, and that they contribute to improved security rather than conflict between communities in competition with one another. Operational plans must also emphasize fostering cooperation between indigenous military forces, police forces, and intelligence services.

Reconstruction and economic development must be closely integrated into security operations to rekindle hope among the population and demonstrate that tangible benefits will flow from their sustained cooperation with counterinsurgent forces. Senior commanders and civil authorities must provide funding and developmental expertise to local commanders and civil-military teams. Programs that jump-start sustainable economic activity and employment, such as agricultural and loan programs, are particularly valuable. Operational-level plans must also identify and advance macro-economic policies that remove obstacles to economic growth (e.g., legal impediments to foreign direct investment, subsidies that discourage entrepreneurship or encourage corruption) and promote a stable economic environment (e.g., low inflation). Plans should also account for international and nongovernmental organizations' development programs to reduce redundancies and identify opportunities for collaboration and burden sharing. If economic improvements are to be sustained, local efforts must be recognized and supported by governmental institutions. For example, a community's effort to build schools will fail unless the education ministry hires teachers, provides educational materials, and allocates funds to sustain the school.

Similarly, local commanders and civil military teams cannot significantly improve local governance or the rule of law if their efforts are not tied to programs at the provincial and national levels. The importance of functioning local governments and the rule of law cannot be overstated; they are essential elements to achieving enduring security. If the government is ineffective, then—despite the best efforts to improve security and move communities toward political accommodation—the pool of popular discontent from which an insurgency draws strength will grow. If communities are unable to count on the government, they tend to fall in on themselves; people turn to religious or tribal leaders, who in turn reinforce particularistic identities that insurgents can exploit. Efforts to improve governmental performance, therefore, must connect the center to the periphery in the areas of policy, public-sector employment, delivery of basic services, infrastructure improvement, and public financial management (i.e., budget formulation and execution). The emphasis in operational planning must be on making indigenous systems work rather than grafting international best practices onto a culture or bureaucratic tradition that is incompatible with them. In short, operational plans must focus on indigenous leaders and systems and connect civil-military efforts at all levels as a means of fostering the functional integration of the indigenous government.[40]

Rule of law, which a comprehensive counterinsurgency plan must integrate into the overall effort, must also receive focused attention from military and civilian officials at the operational level. Senior commanders and civil authorities must work with indigenous governments to help establish a legal framework that allows the government to defeat the insurgency while protecting human rights. The rule of law is a great threat to the insurgent organization; insurgents will attack and intimidate police and judges who uphold and represent it. Thus counterinsurgents must simultaneously build and protect police investigative and judicial capacity. Until security conditions permit the normal functioning of the judicial system, government and counterinsurgency forces must develop a transparent, review-based detainee system that ensures humane treatment. Commanders and senior civilian officials recognize that detention facilities and detainee populations are critical battlegrounds and must help the supported government extend counterinsurgency efforts there to include segregation of leaders, intelligence collection, and rehabilitation prior to release and reintegration. While it is important to ensure that innocents are not imprisoned, it is also important to keep committed insurgents behind bars. As Galula observes, if the counterinsurgent releases insurgents back into a violent environment, "the effects will soon be felt by the policeman, the civil servant, and the soldier."[41]

Effective communication with all relevant parties, especially the indigenous population and the leaders of the supported government and security forces, is also key to winning on the critical battleground of perception. Operational-level commanders, civil authorities, and the local government must be able to explain their intentions, to counter enemy disinformation and propaganda, and to speak up for—and hence bolster the legitimacy of—the government and its security forces. Wherever possible, communications should trace the population's grievance back to the enemy and should expose the enemy's brutality and indifference to the welfare of the population. Decentralization is critical in this area as well, because local political and cultural dynamics (and thus messages associated with them) will vary considerably.

Operational plans must also identify which actions external to the subject country—for example, diplomatic, economic, and international law enforcement efforts—might be critical to the counterinsurgency effort. Often there cannot be an internal solution to an insurgency unless it is reinforced by an external effort to help strengthen the government and isolate the insurgency from support. In general, diplomatic efforts aim to integrate the supported government into the region and enlist the support of reluctant or uncommitted neighbors. Diplomatic or military action might be necessary to convince malign regional actors to desist from activities that undermine the effort.

Ultimately, operational plans must identify long-term, intermediate, and near-term goals in each focus area or line of effort as well as identify the key tasks, programs, and actions necessary to achieve those goals over time. Operational plans should identify specific obstacles to progress and specify how to overcome those obstacles or mitigate their effect. Plans must specify and allocate the resources necessary to accomplish those tasks and affix clear responsibility for them. Near-term goals should contribute to the first priority of achieving sustainable security and stability. Longer-term goals should aim to help transform the society such that the fundamental causes of violence are removed or dramatically reduced. Ideally, actions and programs undertaken in the near term ought to build toward achieving long-term goals.[42] While it is important to keep long-term objectives in mind, it is also important to understand that there may be no long term at all if the supported government is unable to achieve progress in the near term. Plans in each focus area must be integrated to determine which tasks can be undertaken simultaneously and which tasks must be accomplished sequentially. Critical long-term efforts such as civil service reform, the implementation of anticorruption measures, and the development of leaders in the security sector must be initiated early if adequate progress is to be made in time to stabilize the situation.

Directing Counterinsurgency Operations

Successful counterinsurgency operations demand determined, energetic leadership and an integrated civil-military effort. A fragmented, compartmentalized organization will result in an incoherent and ineffective effort.

Because most civilian organizations do not have an operational focus, military officers and NCOs should augment their staff to track and assess the execution of plans. Integration of civil and military efforts frees civilian experts to provide direction and to ensure that solutions are compatible with broader U.S. policy goals, the supported country's culture, and international best practices. Civil-military integration also allows organization by critical line of effort or focus area rather than restricting either soldiers or civilians solely to their own chains of command, and reduces the time that military officers and civilian officials spend talking to each other rather than getting the job done. Integration of civil and military staffs requires each to get out of their cultural comfort zones, but military and civilian leaders must force them to do so. Leadership at the national level will have to help prevent parochialism in Washington from undermining unity of effort. Funding all programs through a single coordinator in Washington—be it in a formalized or ad hoc way—would prove helpful in effecting integration of efforts across departments and their various representatives or attachés.[43]

The integrated civil-military team must be determined to win—that is, to achieve the goals established in the operational plan. Insurgent and terrorist organizations are determined to win, and their standard for success is low. If counterinsurgent organizations are not determined to overcome obstacles, exert influence over key actors, and solve problems, they will be at a severe and perhaps insurmountable disadvantage. Any bureaucratic tendency to regard process as an end in itself must be quashed, and those who lack commitment should be sent home. Operational commanders and senior civilian officials must inspire their staffs to exhibit the same intensity and determination as civilians and soldiers who are working together to defeat the insurgency at the local level. Otherwise, staffs might pursue their own objectives, which sometimes involve protecting their own prerogatives or lessening their burdens. Leaders must encourage their staffs and subordinate leaders to take initiative and undertake actions necessary to accomplish the mission without waiting for orders. Commanders and senior civilian officials must also be willing to underwrite mistakes. Mistakes of commission should be tolerated; passivity should not be tolerated.

Because progress toward objectives is never linear, commanders and civil authorities will need good intelligence and feedback mechanisms to continually reassess the situation holistically and within critical focus areas.

Intelligence must also continually assess the enemy's reactions as the counterinsurgent undertakes the broad range of actions in the plan. While local intelligence analysis focuses on specific enemy organizations as well as the ethnic, tribal, and sectarian dynamics, intelligence efforts at the operational level develop an understanding of how the enemy organization is connected across the country and outside the country. Intelligence estimates should also consider other destabilizing factors that pose a threat to counterinsurgent plans, such as corruption or lack of institutional capacity within the government. Finally, intelligence efforts must concentrate on political dynamics and gain understanding of how malign actors and organizations are attempting to undermine the political strategy or exert influence over government institutions and security forces.

It is especially important to understand how the supported government works and how informal networks within the government are either supporting or undermining the political strategy. Just as military commanders shift boundaries of subordinate units or use mobile forces to target insurgent or terrorist safe havens, senior civilian officials must adjust their influence strategy to deny the enemy critical space in the political domain. Senior officials must work with cooperative members of the supported government to isolate those who are providing cover for illegal armed groups, are involved in corruption that undermines the government's ability to provide services, or are pursuing a particularistic agenda that undermines security and the political strategy.

The need for a holistic assessment—and constant reassessments—cannot be overstated. Commanders and senior civilian officials must also be aware that systems analysis can create an illusion of control and create the illusion of progress in counterinsurgency operations. Metrics designed to measure progress often tell commanders and civilian officials how they are executing their plan (e.g. money spent, numbers of indigenous forces trained and equipped, districts or provinces transferred to indigenous control), but fail to highlight logical disconnects that sometimes allow leaders to confuse activity with progress toward achieving policy goals. Estimates of the situation, therefore, often underestimate the enemy and other sources of instability and these estimates, in turn, serve as a foundation for plans that are inconsistent with the nature of the conflict. An overreliance on metrics can lead to a tendency to develop short-term solutions for long-term problems and a focus on simplistic charts rather than on a deliberate examination of questions and issues critical to the war effort. Because of the variation in conditions at the local level, much of the data that is aggregated at the national level is of little utility.

But if it is vital to maintain a holistic estimate of the situation, it is also important to remain sensitive to unique dynamics at the local level. Whenever possible, operational commanders, senior officials, and their staffs should travel to gain an appreciation for local problems and ensure that subordinate units and civil-military teams have the resources they need and that they understand how their efforts are intended to fit into the overall counterinsurgency effort. Operational-level staffs should collaborate with subordinate units during planning and periodic assessments. The situation and experience at the local level may represent an opportunity or a danger that may require the modification of operational plans and priorities. Learning and adapting are critical to success because the interaction with the enemy and other destabilizing factors ensures that progress in counterinsurgency is anything but linear.

The requirement to adapt quickly to unforeseen conditions means that commanders and civil-military teams at all levels require additional forces and resources that can be committed to seize upon opportunities or protect against dangers; there must be reserves of forces and resources. Emphasis in planning and directing operations must be on effectiveness rather than efficiency. The complexity and uncertainty of counterinsurgency requires a certain degree of redundancy and spare capacity as well as decentralization. The assumption of near-certainty in war delivered by operational net assessment, combined with the linear thinking associated with concepts like effects-based operations, led to the belief that forces and resources required could be calculated with a great deal of precision. Planners still captured by the flawed thinking of the 1990s might endeavor to commit just enough force and just enough resources to achieve objectives, establish security, and help nascent governments and security forces assume responsibility for the counterinsurgency effort. A bias toward making the minimum necessary effort creates opportunities for and cedes the initiative to the enemy. Moreover, efficiency in all forms of warfare, including counterinsurgency, means barely winning. And in war, barely winning is an ugly proposition.

Conclusion

The concept of mission command, that is, the conduct of military operations through decentralized execution based upon mission orders, clearly applies to counterinsurgency operations. Decentralizing operations without adequate preparation, sound and comprehensive operational planning, and vigorous direction, however, is likely to achieve only transitory or very limited success. Decentralized operations place heavy demands on small units and junior leaders; senior commanders must prepare soldiers and leaders for those demands through training and education. Counterinsurgency efforts at the local level must be consistent with an operational concept that integrates those efforts and directs them toward clearly defined goals. Operational commanders and senior civilian officials must ensure unity of effort within their own civil-military organization and among their organization, coalition nations, and the supported government. All efforts must support policy goals and a political strategy that aims to defeat the enemy and strengthen the supported government and security forces.

While directing counterinsurgency operations, operational commanders and senior civilian officials must continually reassess the situation, make necessary adjustments, and ensure that all members of their team take initiative to overcome obstacles in pursuit of mission accomplishment. New and emerging technologies can contribute significantly to the execution of mission command in counterinsurgency operations. Communications and information technologies, however, should be employed in a way that permits effective decentralization of operations rather than as means for centralizing control of resources and decision making.

4

The Air Force and Twenty-First-Century Conflicts: Dysfunctional or Dynamic?

Charles J. Dunlap, Jr.

Tanks and armor are not a big deal—the planes are the killers. I can handle everything but the jet fighters.[1]

—TALIBAN COMMANDER, June 2008

When we hear the planes overhead, we feel relief because we know it is going to be over, and we are probably not going to die that day.[2]

—U.S. ARMY SERGEANT, September 2008

In the twenty-first century, perspective matters. To America's adversaries in the field, U.S. air capabilities, including those of the U.S. Air Force, are a terrifying threat, far more intimidating than many other elements of American power. From the perspective of an American infantryman in the midst of combat, airpower is a psychological—not only a physical—lifesaver.

Yet in the salons of newspapers, think tanks, and academia, and even among its sister services and other government entities, the air force is the gang that can't shoot straight. During the same month in which the Taliban

The views and opinions expressed herein are those of the author alone, and not necessarily those of the Department of Defense or any of its components.

commander quoted in the epigraph gave his rather strong testimonial about the effectiveness of airpower, the editors of the *Washington Post* derided the air force as "adrift,"[3] and those of the *New York Times* condemned it as "dysfunctional." Functionality, it seems, is much a matter of perspective.[4]

Notwithstanding success on actual battlefields, the U.S. Air Force finds itself suffering setbacks in the all-important area of operation that is Washington. Already battered by allegations of improprieties in awarding contracts, and beset with difficulties in communicating its purpose and vision, the service staggered under revelations that nuclear-related materials had been mishandled. As the incidents were interpreted as failures of leadership, the air force's secretary and chief of staff were ousted, and other senior leaders suffered career-ending accountability actions.[5]

More fundamentally, however, the Air Force's sense of itself is under siege. As the service that prides itself on its ability to keep the world's most dangerous existential threats at bay, it nevertheless is finding that contemporary defense thinking undervalues that ability. Indeed, it has never been more fashionable to discount the need for the kind of firepower the Air Force best provides and to mock the very suggestion that we are likely to do battle against another modern army—let alone an air force. Even Secretary of Defense Robert Gates categorized apprehensions about such possibilities as "next-war-itis."[6]

With few airpower advocates in the Office of the Secretary of Defense,[7] it is not surprising that the National Defense Strategy, issued in June of 2008, perpetuated an approach to national security planning which heavily emphasizes "irregular war," epitomized by the conflicts in Iraq and Afghanistan.[8] While acknowledging the notion of hedging against the emergence of a peer-competitor, the document unmistakably focuses on conflicts with nonstate actors at the lower end of the spectrum of conflict. Specifically, it states that "for the foreseeable future, winning the Long War against violent extremist movements will be the central objective of the U.S."[9]

Unless airmen can do a better job of explaining to decision makers how air, space, and cyberspace power provides potent, *full-spectrum* capabilities to the joint team, the focus of the National Defense Strategy does not spell good news for the Air Force.[10] In popular imagination, not to mention the minds of key leaders, waging irregular warfare against extremism is overwhelmingly the province of the ground forces. Fueling this view are the heretofore rarely challenged assumptions about Field Manual (FM) 3-24, the army and Marine Corps counterinsurgency (COIN) doctrine issued in December 2006.[11] Specifically, there is a widespread belief that principles enunciated in FM 3-24 were wholly responsible for suppressing violence in Iraq.

Of course, as I will go on to show, there is strong empirical data demonstrating that airpower was, in fact, vital to the joint success in Iraq beginning in 2007. But that evidence has not penetrated very far into the public consciousness. The belief that the manual is the *sine qua non* of COIN is significant—if not alarming—for the air force, since the doctrine conceives of only a very limited role for airpower, confining its discussion largely to a five-page annex. Consequently, many wrongly believe that airpower has little relevance to the current wars in Iraq and Afghanistan.

More disconcerting is that, to the extent airpower is employed to fight insurgencies, many believe it is actually undermining the supposedly all-important centerpiece of counterinsurgency, that is, winning "hearts and minds."[12] In so concluding, they point to reports in the summer of 2008 that air strikes in Afghanistan were responsible for needless civilian deaths. To their way of thinking, the military can prevent such casualties by restraining the use of airpower in favor of more U.S. ground troops.[13]

All of this combines to create an atmosphere so poisoned that some pundits question the very rationale for having an air force.[14] The irony of the situation is that more than any other service, the air force has dominated the physical domains in which it operates. While the ground forces still struggle in Iraq and Afghanistan to defeat lightly armed insurgents whom they typically greatly outnumber, the U.S. Air Force has made short work of every aerial opponent it has faced, including top-of-the-line Russian-built aircraft in Serbia. For its part, Saddam Hussein's air force was so petrified of facing American pilots that it literally buried its airplanes to avoid doing so.

The purpose of this essay is to outline several of the sources of the Air Force's difficulties, discuss some Air Force successes, and offer a few thoughts for the way ahead. It is uncompromising on one point: if the Air Force's critics succeed in deconstructing the world's most successful military force, the security of the United States will be in real jeopardy.

Air Force Culture and Leadership Development

Identifying the underlying cause of the Air Force's problematic state is no easy task. As would be the case with any large and complicated organization, there are multiple causes for the service's current institutional difficulties. Still, it is always useful to examine leadership development when an organization is not meeting its own expectations or those of others. This examination suggests that the Air Force's leadership development process and its institutional culture intertwine in a way that may not be best serving its interests in the twenty-first century.

Let us begin with the current situation: it is indisputable that the Air Force has relatively few senior officers filling the leadership posts deemed most influential in national security policymaking.[15] Equally troubling is that the service has few flag officers able to act in the larger defense community as effective spokespersons and advocates for airpower.[16]

Likewise, the Air Force has not—as the army has—produced a cadre of warrior-intellectuals.[17] Rare is the Air Force general who combines front-line combat experience with a broad-based PhD. In other words, the Air Force simply does not have combined in a single senior officer the qualities that have helped to make army general David H. Petraeus so successful and so widely admired as the prototype of military leadership for the twenty-first century.

The career path of most airmen makes it difficult to mirror the background of a Petraeus. The relatively lengthy training undertaken by aviators (who form the core of the service's senior leadership) leaves little time for the advanced study required for a PhD. Beyond an initial year of undergraduate pilot training, officers must continually fly to stay current in the increasingly complex aircraft used by today's Air Force. Over a career, the weeks and months of training needed to maintain essentially the same flying skills a company grade officer uses detract from the time available to acquire the kind of education most important at the senior level.

The result is that few who go on to command major Air Force organizations have a doctorate on their résumé. Of course, there are many well-educated officers in the Air Force. More than half have a postgraduate degree,[18] and most flag officers have at least a master's degree in some specialty. The Air Force does continue to "churn out scores of airmen with advanced degrees," as the former secretary of the Air Force recently observed, but many of the advanced degrees are in science and engineering.[19] Indeed, a study by Colonel Tom Ruby points out the "relative paucity" of Air Force senior officers "with doctorates applicable to strategy development."[20]

The emphasis on the hard sciences colors the outlook of many Air Force officers on a variety of issues to a point where it much defines the culture of the service. Although the in-depth knowledge of these officers enables them to understand the intricacies of the many advanced systems the Air Force employs, it can put them at a disadvantage in a world in which the skills of the liberally educated are increasingly valued in leadership positions. Nor does the assignment process close the gap. One study argues that airmen do not compete well for major theater commands because they have "a narrower upbringing and less exposure to the political process than other service members."[21]

Again, Air Force culture plays a role in accentuating this deficiency. Beyond the training demands that keep them in the cockpit, the sheer love of flying creates a dislike for the developmental staff jobs so essential to the leadership of twenty-first century militaries. For instance, most experts agree that effective military strategy must take into account a range of political, social, moral, and economic matters in addition to those purely military in nature.[22] The narrower upbringing of Air Force officers often does not allow them to internalize adequately these important disciplines, and leaves them with a tendency to analyze problems from a scientific and technological perspective, which can in turn make them less adept at integrating the other important factors into their thinking.

Air force thinking does devote much intellectual energy to examining and optimizing the characteristics of its technologies, as well as the mechanics of procuring and maintaining them. However, creatively envisioning the strategic employment of air, space, and cyberspace power gets markedly less attention. Put another way, the Air Force is culturally more interested in encyclopedic knowledge of the specifications of its equipment than in how to best use that equipment across the spectrum of conflict. That the late Carl Builder identified virtually the same problem in the early 1990s only serves to underline how entrenched it is culturally.[23]

For all the technical expertise of airmen, some officers argue that today's Air Force suffers from anti-intellectualism, that is, from "valuing doers over thinkers."[24] According to Colonel Ruby, "Technical proficiency cannot substitute for an ability to analyze issues critically and apply every asset available to achieve a specific end in differing political and military contexts."[25] This suggests another issue that bedevils the Air Force: the science and engineering propensities of airmen render them less than fully sensitive to the human dimension of the art of war making.

This insensitivity can harm the Air Force in unexpected ways. For example, the Air Force's concept of centralized control and decentralized execution of airpower has led to an unfortunate assumption by its comrades in arms, particularly in the army. The Air Force relies on advanced communications methodologies that permit the comprehensive command and control of its capabilities from a single air and space operations center in a given theater of operations.[26] Typically, the operations center is physically separate from the operations center of the overall joint force commander. Thus senior Air Force commanders were not co-located with the overall joint force commander in either Iraq or Afghanistan. Theoretical efficiencies aside, the physical absence of Air Force flag officers from the councils of war conducted by army and Marine Corps generals in Iraq and Afghanistan prevented the development of the kind of personal bonds that produce mutual respect and understanding. Moreover, it seems to have created suspicion among some ground-component officers that the Air Force lacks sufficient understanding of or, worse, concern about, their needs.

The failure to fully appreciate the importance of developing these personal bonds does not bode well for the future. Compared to the army and the Marine Corps, the Air Force has far fewer officers destined for senior rank with extended service in either Iraq or Afghanistan. Many top Air Force officers who have served in the Middle East did so at the site of the air operations center or at another airbase located outside of those countries. As a practical matter, as Iraq and Afghanistan veterans assume higher leadership positions in the army and Marine Corps, this divergence in experience may create further difficulties for the Air Force in its relationship with the ground forces.

Likewise, it may be hard to place Air Force officers, however otherwise talented, in positions of prominence either in joint commands or in key positions in the Office of the Secretary of Defense. Understandably, those with service in Iraq or Afghanistan will likely be favored since they will presumably be more cognizant of the nuances of contemporary conflicts. This will result in combatant commands responsible for the areas of probable conflict dominated by officers not in the Air Force. Because of the extraordinary—and growing—authority of these four-star joint commands, the absence of airmen from the upper ranks of the most important ones is worrisome for those who believe that the air weapon has an irreplaceable role to play in protecting the nation's interests.

Today, there is a growing tendency for combatant commanders, emboldened by supportive Defense Department polices, to attempt to expand their authority at the expense of individual services. Consider, for example, the effort by Marine Corps general James N. Mattis, the commander of Joint Forces Command, to expunge the concept of effects-based operations (EBO) even though it is fundamental to Air Force doctrine.[27] There are many arguments for and against EBO, but suffice it to say that at its core, EBO focuses on achieving certain effects desired by the commander without particular concern for which service or platform accomplishes the necessary tasks.[28]

To be sure, it is possible that the Marines could consider EBO a threat to their air-ground task force approach.[29] For example, the implementation of EBO might require making all aviation assets available for theater-wide tasking based upon the joint force commander's highest priorities—that is, airpower would not be reserved for use at the corps' discretion. In that case, the Marines could see EBO as disrupting the air-ground synergy that they believe their style of warfare requires, and hence as undermining the combat power of Marine formations to the detriment of the overall effort.

Regardless, for a combatant commander to use his joint authority to attempt to demolish another service's operational approach is, to say the least, unprecedented. Retired Air Force lieutenant general Thomas McInerney termed General Mattis's memo "parochial, un-joint, biased, one-sided," and pointed out further that EBO had been "key in the transformation of warfare—and proven in the most successful U.S. military conflicts of the past 20 years (Desert Storm and Allied Force)."[30] Yet such bureaucratic eviscerations of Air Force doctrine are what happen when too few airmen occupy key joint billets, and—importantly—when the service is perceived as vulnerable.

Additionally, the Air Force's "engineering" mind-set tends to generate a rather naïve belief that the efficacy of its capabilities are self-evident. Many airmen seem to assume that decision makers will readily engage in a dispassionate, almost mathematical analysis of available data, which will irrefutably demonstrate the utility and value of airpower and the Air Force. In such a conception of the world, advocacy per se is wholly unnecessary and, indeed, a bit unseemly. In the real world, of course, advocating particular policies or arguing for alternatives requires a far more aggressive approach than merely computing numbers and presenting spreadsheets. The numbers do not, necessarily, speak for themselves.

All of this is in stark contrast to what the other services have mastered. The army's development of FM 3-24 is a classic example of savvy twenty-first-century policymaking. During the developmental stage of the doctrine, the army invited comment from a range of representatives from outside the military, including the media, academia, and think tanks.[31] The army drafters of the manual gave the inputs from these unconventional sources more than just a respectful hearing; in many instances their suggestions were wholly adopted.

It is not surprising, therefore, that the final document was praised for the very characteristics so admired by some civilian intellectuals and academics—notwithstanding the opaqueness of these characteristics in terms of military doctrine.[32] As one commentator explained, FM 3-24 was popular

> among sections of the country's liberal-minded intelligentsia. This was warfare for northeastern graduate students—complex, blended with politics, designed to build countries rather than destroy them, and fashioned to minimize violence. It was a doctrine with particular appeal to people who would never own a gun.[33]

What this process did, in effect, was to disarm potential adversaries—those ordinarily likely to oppose almost anything coming out of the armed forces—by giving them intellectual ownership of the doctrine produced. This generated an outpouring of flattery from a myriad of unusual venues, including an almost obsequious review in the *New York Times Book Review*.[34]

Much of what the manual was understood to advocate was not, in fact, what proved successful in Iraq during the period of its supposed implementation in 2007 and 2008;[35] but its public perception as calling for a "kinder and gentler" form of war making with little use for airpower remains firmly in place. At least insofar as FM 3-24's reputation for passivity is concerned, it seems to be more a product of the wishful thinking of some of the manual's fans than the machinations of its drafters. General Petraeus, one of the manual's principal authors, insists that it does not "shy away from the need to kill the enemy" and that "the words 'kill' and 'capture' are on every page."[36]

Nevertheless, respected trade publications such as *Defense News* were claiming as late as September of 2008 that the "Army and Marines are succeeding in Iraq, thanks to a softer approach."[37] Regardless of what the manual does or does not say, the much-derided techniques of "killing and capturing" both spiked during this most successful period of the Iraq War, and—importantly—airpower became key to that effort as air strikes increased fivefold in 2007.[38] Retired Air Force lieutenant general Michael Dunn, the president of the Air Force Association, characterized the counterinsurgency effort in this way in July of 2008:

> The so-called troop surge has really been an airpower surge. Consider this. Air sorties are up 85%; air strikes are up 400%; weight of ordnance dropped is up 1000%. Some insiders say that 90% of the terrorists being killed are being killed by airpower.[39]

Notwithstanding the enormous role airpower played (and continues to play) in counterinsurgency operations, the *Washington Post* accurately observes that the "public faces of the wars in Iraq and Afghanistan have been almost exclusively those of troops in Army and Marine Corps uniforms."[40] Thus, the army, despite years of botched strategies (as recorded in such books as Tom Ricks's *Fiasco*[41]), has been able to reinvent its "brand" to be that of an intellectual, forward-thinking institution.

To meet its larger manpower recruiting need and facilitate this transformational rebranding, the army enjoys a significantly larger advertising budget than that of the Air Force. Beyond its paltry marketing budget, the Air Force has been burdened with its problematic "Above All" advertising campaign, which viewers have found alternatively inscrutable and arrogant.[42] While all service advertising efforts seek to appeal to recruits by projecting a sense of organizational uniqueness and excellence, the Air Force's slogan turned out to be self-defeating. It is almost (but not quite) understandable that the Air Force frequently has found itself denounced as an organization wedded to outdated Cold War concepts.[43]

The army (and the Marine Corps) have also benefited from scores of books, articles, and broadcasts that—whatever their view of the leadership—treated the individual soldier or marine with great sympathy. The reason is easy to discern: those who produced the most favorable commentary usually had been embedded with ground units. The army's own study of the Iraq war, *On Point II*, recognizes the effect this had by quoting *Los Angeles Times* reporter John Hendren:

> When you're living in tents with these guys and eating what they eat and cleaning the dirt off the glasses, it's a whole different experience. You definitely have a concern about knowing people so well that you sympathize with them.[44]

On Point II downplays the phenomenon by insisting rather illogically that the reporting of embedded journalists was not biased, even though the authors came to "understand the Soldiers with whom they lived *and who protected them from danger*."[45] In truth, there is little doubt that the association with the vibrant personalities of America's young soldiers and marines who were protecting them from very real threats was influential, and this "understanding" boosted the ground services' image overall.

The Air Force has little hope of engendering favorable press the same way. The nature of the service's operations is such that it does not lend itself to the embedding of reporters. Embeds rarely find themselves in the cockpit of an airplane[46] or, for that matter, in the confines of an unmanned aerial system (UAS) or satellite. It is quite rare for an airman to have a human-interest story related to Air Force capabilities that is as captivating as that of his infantry counterpart fighting amid the sights, sounds, and smells of ground combat.

Regrettably, to the extent there are human-interest stories about airpower coming out of the wars in Iraq and Afghanistan, they are typically negative ones, emphasizing the tragedy of civilian deaths. Air Force "stories" tend to revolve around technology rather than people. Given the relative paucity of authors with the interest and background to write animatedly about the technology that underpins the Air Force way of war, the service's difficulties in explaining itself are not hard to understand.

In certain respects, the Air Force has been its own worst enemy. Beginning with the distribution of videos of precision bombs falling into air-shafts during the first Gulf War, the service has created the perception that what it does is easy. In every conflict for more than half a century, the Air Force has provided near-perfect air defense as well as long-range strikes and theater and strategic lift; as a result, the service garners little thought or consideration by its beneficiaries. The U.S. national defense community cavalierly considers these resources as givens, though of course virtually no other air force in the world can provide these capabilities.

The situation is even more aggravated with respect to costly and intricate space systems. Here, too, Air Force capabilities are taken for granted. The Secretary of the Air Force recently noted that in the Middle East, "U.S. and Coalition forces are supported by over 46 satellites, along with their network of operations centers and ground stations, operated by airmen at bases across the globe."[47] Yet the Air Force's sister services seem at best to recognize only vaguely that these are Air Force–furnished resources.

Beyond being taken for granted, the Air Force also must deal with the perception that its high-tech weaponry is easier to control than is really the case. Consider this statement by a former member of the National Security Council:

> Air power is more susceptible to legal and policy adjustment than ground combat, in light of the variations in means and method of attack available through variation in munitions, delivery azimuth, angle of attack, aim point, fuse, and explosive, all amplified with the assistance of computer simulation.[48]

This type of overstatement, which implies that Air Force weaponry is perfectly controllable, exacerbates criticism when things seem to go awry. There is little appreciation for the vagaries of combat; the assumption is that any unintended result is due to malfeasance.

The air force has not effectively conveyed the vulnerability of the current force or, equally important, the fragility of the supporting industrial base. Although key decision makers seem cognizant of the service's aging fleet, they evidently believe the looming deficiencies do not merit immediate attention. Accordingly, decisions concerning the production of the F-22 fighter and the acquisition of a new tanker were left to the new administration.[49]

Even respected experts like Professor Richard K. Betts of Columbia University appear to misapprehend the lead time required to manufacture and field air, space, and cyberspace technology. Betts argues that hedging against a peer-competitor threat like China merely requires a "mobilization strategy."[50] By this he means putting off the production of weaponry "until genuine evidence" exists that military supremacy is slipping.[51] But waiting until the threat actually exists is often waiting too long to produce successful counters. Consider how long it took to field the relatively low-tech Mine Resistant Ambush Protected (MRAP) vehicles.[52]

Apparently, Professor Betts—and presumably other national security experts—are unaware that once the production line for a high-tech weapon like an advanced aircraft terminates, it may take years to regenerate it. There is no "mobilization strategy" that is meaningful for a service that depends upon superior technology for its military effectiveness. Once a threat is actually materializing, it is most likely too late to address it by the manufacture of new equipment. To paraphrase an erstwhile defense leader, "you go to war with the air force you have; not the one you want."

An Airpower Renaissance?

Do all of these issues mean the Air Force is doomed to be underappreciated and underresourced, and hence undervalued as an instrument of national power? Actually, no. Despite its many ills, airpower—if not the Air Force itself—is enjoying a renaissance of sorts. Rather surprisingly, this is nowhere more evident than in counterinsurgency operations.

The details of the revolutionary changes that have made airpower such a capability of choice in counterinsurgency operations are available elsewhere. Suffice it to say here that airpower "persistence and precision" technologies—many of which have been only recently fielded— have led influential strategists to insist that the nature of warfare has fundamentally changed. In the fall of 2007, retired army general Barry McCaffrey observed:

> We have already made a 100 year war-fighting leap-ahead with MQ-1 Predator, MQ-9 Reaper, and Global Hawk. Now we have loiter times in excess of 24 hours, persistent eyes on target, micro-kill with Hellfire and 500 lb JDAM bombs, synthetic aperture radar, and a host of ISR [intelligence, surveillance, and reconnaissance] sensors and communications potential that have fundamentally changed the nature of warfare.[53]

In essence, profound advances in the ability to conduct persistent and precise ISR, complemented by the availability of precise strikes, have combined to create a new way of war, one that is increasingly problematic for low-tech insurgents to counter. Perhaps even more importantly, these new high-tech capabilities make it possible for airpower to have a strategic effect not on civilian morale, as airpower pioneers once sought, but on the minds of the *actual combatants*.[54]

As the first of the epigraphs to this chapter suggests, today airpower can inflict on insurgents a sense of helplessness that is psychologically debilitating. Commanders seem to understand this development. According to counterinsurgency expert Colin Kahl, air strikes in Iraq increased dramatically in 2007 partly because of the realization of their ability to affect the enemy's psychology.[55] In fact, hints about the psychological effect of precision aerial fires had appeared even earlier. General Tommy Franks relates that during his tenure in command, an Afghan ally told him that the AC-130 gunship is "a famous airplane [whose] guns have *destroyed the spirit* of the Taliban and the Arabs."[56]

The psychological unhinging of today's insurgents by contemporary airpower is apparent in more than just the battlespaces of Iraq and Afghanistan. The Revolutionary Armed Force of Colombia (FARC, in its Spanish acronym), the main insurgent group in Colombia, is being devastated by desertions which, according to interviews with former rebels, are much motivated by "the sheer terror of being bombed by Colombian fighter planes."[57]

In American counterinsurgency operations, the phenomenal growth of robotic aeronautical platforms makes it possible to achieve almost Pavlovian psychological reactions. As one report put it:

> Iraqi insurgents have learned to fear the drones. "They hear some sort of air noise and they don't know exactly what it is, but they know it's associated with 'my buddy getting killed,'" says [a U.S. soldier].[58]

The sheer inability to defend against airpower no doubt contributes to its devastating psychological effect, as insurgents have few weapons capable of holding high-performance aircraft at risk.[59] In fact, the greatest threat to airpower in counterinsurgency operations is not a weapon at all, but rather misperceptions about its relationship to civilian casualties, especially in Afghanistan.

The Civilian Casualty Conundrum

It is, of course, true that aerial fires—like ground-based fires—can cause civilian causalities.[60] However, there is no question that Taliban and al Qaeda are stepping up their sophisticated effort to turn every tragedy into a political issue.[61] Unfortunately, they are enjoying significant success. According to the chief NATO spokesman, the coalition "is definitely not winning the information war."[62] Part of the problem is clearly bureaucratic. As the *Washington Post* explains: "Although civilian deaths have been frequent and real, officials say that the Taliban quickly broadcasts exaggerated tolls, stoking public anger, while foreign military officers may take days to respond."[63]

There is a real risk that the Taliban may succeed in pressuring coalition forces to virtually abandon airpower. Misinformation is playing a role. Friendly forces do not seem to understand that it is not wise to declare that every civilian death, however tragic, is the product of an error. Too often, however, they seem to do just that. For example, the commander of NATO's International Security Assistance Force in Afghanistan recently insisted that "any civilian casualty caused by NATO or American forces is inadvertent."[64] This statement, together with earlier NATO statements suggesting that no bombing would take place if it were known that civilians were in the area, can create serious military difficulties.[65]

International law prohibits targeting civilians, but it does not ban attacks on legitimate targets even if it is known that innocents will be killed as a result. Rather, the law requires only that such losses not be "excessive" in relation to the military advantage sought.[66] If the law were otherwise, it would simply encourage adversaries to use innocent civilians as human shields.[67]

Of course, every effort must be made to limit civilian losses, but the requisite analysis ought to take into account those civilians who may be killed by Taliban and al Qaeda *if these groups are allowed to escape an airstrike*. Limiting civilian casualties requires as careful an assessment of the consequences of *not* bombing as of the bombing itself. When civilian deaths occur in the course of an otherwise legitimate attack because the enemy is wrongly intermingling with civilians, the legal and moral responsibility for the deaths is upon the insurgents, not the attackers. Counterinsurgency forces would do well to make that clear to decision makers and the public.

Somewhat surprisingly, there seems to be a rather widespread belief that more ground-force counterinsurgents will somehow reduce the number of civilian casualties. The evidence indicates otherwise. The air strikes that have recently caused the most civilian casualties were typically not pre-planned in the air operations center, but were the product of actions taken at the behest of U.S. forces on the ground.[68] Such strikes can lack the detailed vetting that otherwise takes place in the operations center targeting cell. As one journalist observes, such planning may include extended aerial surveillance that provides those in the operations center with "a better vantage point than an Army unit has just down the street from a group of insurgents."[69]

When airpower is applied as the result of this kind of preplanning, even Human Rights Watch activist Marc Garlasoc concedes that "airstrikes probably are the most discriminating weapon that exists."[70] However, when they are called for by troops on the ground, "not all air strikes can be so meticulously planned." This is the view of General James Conway, commandant of the Marines, who points out that "U.S. or allied units can call in sudden strikes when they find themselves in a firefight or stumble on a meeting of Taliban leaders." He also makes clear how insurgents exploit the imprecision of these unplanned attacks: "Sometimes it's a conscious tactic of these people who meet to make sure there are kids playing in the compound so that they're seen, and that complicates your targeting methodology. . . . This is a dirty game being played."[71]

In any event, troops on the ground do not necessarily equate to more discriminate targeting. Journalist Mark Thompson—a frequent critic of airpower—admitted after a ground force raid that reportedly left as many as fifteen civilians dead that "having American soldiers in a position to call in strikes is no guarantee that civilians won't be killed."[72]

More troops on the ground mean more risk against which the air weapon may be the sole defensive recourse. This is especially so in Afghanistan, where the mountainous terrain leaves few other options for isolated garrisons undergoing unanticipated attacks that threaten to overrun them. The desire to attack without the threat of retaliation by air may well be a principal motivation for the Taliban's propaganda efforts to delegitimize airpower.[73]

Airpower and COIN

Although it is unquestionably true that military means cannot alone achieve all the goals of a counterinsurgency effort, it is also accurate to say that in terms of suppressing violence, the strategy of "killing and capturing," as noted above, has proven more effective than expected. This strategy was presumed to rely on deployment of massive numbers of U.S. ground forces as counterinsurgents. FM 3-24, for example, calls for a "minimum troop density" of twenty counterinsurgents per thousand residents;[74] it was such calculations that led to the "surge" of nearly thirty thousand American troops into Iraq in 2007.

However, recent reports call into question the "more boots on the ground" theory. Specifically, journalist Bob Woodward, author of the *The War Within* (about the surge phase of the Iraq War), insists that "at least three other factors were as important as, or even more important than, the surge" including operations that "locate, target and kill key individuals" in various insurgent groups.[75]

This is a very significant truth for developing counterinsurgency strategy for the United States because it is becoming increasingly clear that deploying masses of *American* troops will always be problematic in irregular warfare situations, and especially so in the Middle East. Studies demonstrate that the presence of foreign forces nearly always invigorates an insurgency. The "fundamental motivation" for insurgencies generally, expert William R. Polk maintains, is "to protect the integrity of the native group from foreigners."[76] This is especially so in Iraq.[77]

Thus the desirability of airpower, which does not require a large "footprint" in a nation suffering from an insurgency, and perhaps requires none at all. This is not an especially new feature of the air weapon. What is new is the capacity to "target and kill" specific individuals, the exact capability Woodward says was so important in suppressing violence in Iraq. Consider this report from journalist Mark Benjamin:

> The Air Force recently watched one man in Iraq for more than five weeks, carefully recording his habits—where he lives, works and worships, and whom he meets. . . . The military may decide to have such a man arrested, or to do nothing at all. Or, at any moment they could decide to blow him to smithereens.[78]

Similarly, the *Los Angeles Times* reported in April of 2008 that NATO forces in Afghanistan "recently have had unusual success in tracking and targeting mid-level Taliban field commanders, killing scores of them in pinpoint airstrikes."[79] Cases like this suggest that neutralizing individual insurgents is much more important to overall counterinsurgency success than FM 3-24 and other approaches would indicate.

The need for a counterinsurgency strategy that does not require large numbers of U.S. ground forces is very great. According to James S. Corum, the loss of blood and treasure in Iraq has so eroded domestic support for similar operations elsewhere that they are unlikely in the future, "no matter how necessary or justified they might be."[80] Polls seem to bear this out. Even though the percentage of Americans who think the United States can win the war in Iraq rose to 58 percent in August of 2008, the percentage opposing the war also rose to 60 percent—as did the percentage who thought the United States made a mistake to send troops to Iraq in the first place.[81]

Is Imitation Flattery or . . . ?

Perhaps the greatest endorsement of the efficacy of airpower in counter-insurgency operations might be expressed in the maxim, "Imitation is the greatest form of flattery." Although airpower is seldom given much credit by the ground forces, it appears to some observers that the army nevertheless wants to build, in effect, its own air force.[82] The army's acquisition of the Sky Warrior, a virtual replica of the Air Force's Predator unmanned aerial system, is but one piece of evidence among several that gives credence to this charge.[83]

Another more graphic indicator came in June of 2008. Thom Shanker of the *New York Times* reported that the army, charging the Air Force with irrelevance and an inability to meet its requests for "sophisticated surveillance aircraft," was developing its own aviation unit.[84] The *Wall Street Journal* later revealed that the "army is preparing to deploy a network of drones and other surveillance aircraft to Afghanistan."[85] All of this is a tacit admission by the ground forces themselves that airpower has revolutionized counterinsurgency warfare, and that airpower is vastly more efficient and effective than certain manpower-intensive infantry modalities of the past.

At the same time, there is little to suggest that ground forces understand and employ airpower more productively than does the Air Force. Consider that in Afghanistan, dubious army airpower planning for Operation Anaconda would have produced a disaster had not air force fixed-wing assets rescued the operation.[86] Virtually the only conventional victory the Iraqi military achieved in 2003, moreover, was the defeat of an army Apache helicopter unit that left twenty-seven of thirty-three helicopters unable to fly.[87] Also telling, as Major Robert J. Seifert points out in a *Joint Forces Quarterly* article, is how inefficiently ground commanders in Iraq used the AC-130 gunships; indeed, their strategy was disturbingly reminiscent of one that proved so ineffective in North Africa during World War II.[88] The commanders limited the aircraft to providing air cover to specific units, and this made the gunships unavailable to attack emerging targets in another unit's area of operations. They failed to optimize each sortie by refusing to link the "on call" aircraft to several units, thus making it unable to respond to the one with the greatest need.[89]

All of this makes some of the official writings of senior army officers quite curious. Army lieutenant general Michael Vane asserts in *Defense*

News that only soldiers at the "lowest echelon" (and not, he supposes, those at "25,000 feet or 10 miles off-shore") can "find, capture, and if necessary, kill" today's "religious extremists and nonstate actors."[90] Thus he claims that land power "needs more of [the] budget pie" than the other services. In another article, however, then–Lieutenant General Raymond T. Odierno claims that aerial intelligence, surveillance, and reconnaissance (as opposed to soldiers at the "lowest echelon") are essential for today's counterinsurgency operations—and that these should be under a ground force commander's control.[91]

In any event, it seems clear that airpower has, rather unexpectedly, emerged as *the* capability of choice for *the* counterinsurgency fight. One need look no further than the fact that intelligence, surveillance, and reconnaissance assets were General Petraeus's "top hardware priority in Iraq."[92] Would it be efficient to give additional aerial platforms to the army officers who complain that the Air Force is not filling enough of their requests for surveillance aircraft? Not likely. Because the Air Force conducts "split operations"—employing pilots in the United States to control large numbers of forward-deployed unmanned aircaft—it is able to keep 88 percent of these unmanned planes operational.[93] The army, however, can organize itself to deploy only about 30 percent of its unmanned aerial assets at any given time.[94]

In truth, *joint* warfare is most powerful when individual services focus upon their core competencies. In a world where thousands of airmen are filling army billets because of shortages in ground force personnel, it makes no sense for a service to try to replicate the special capabilities of another service. Such duplication is not just unnecessarily costly; it also detracts from the combat power that interdependence might otherwise provide. Moreover, viewing the allocation of scarce resources as a scramble for slices of the "budget pie" is profoundly unhelpful in preparing to meet the challenges of twenty-first-century conflicts.

The Future

Despite the Air Force's current difficulties, the future of the service is bright if for no other reason than that airpower itself has demonstrated extraordinary flexibility and utility across the spectrum of conflict. The recent innovative and decisive applications of range airpower platforms in counterinsurgency settings are powerful indicators of the resilience of this central feature of the air weapon. That said, there is no doubt that the Air Force has much work to do if it is to become—and to be perceived as—a more effective and respected member of the joint team.

At the fall 2008 meeting of the Air Force Association, General Norton Schwartz, Air Force chief of staff, alluded to an important principle seemingly overlooked by too many of today's strategists—that is, that technology can allow the aerial warfighter to be far from the fight and still be essential to mission success. General Schwartz insisted, "The value of an Airman's contribution is not measured by his or her proximity to the target. . . . In fact, without [the airmen's] expertise, *no one* would be near the target."[95] General Schwartz's point is that, notwithstanding the emotion the close fight may engender, the purpose of using force is to achieve certain effects, and to do so with the least risk to human beings. Airpower carries the most potential to achieve desired effects with the lowest risk.The real value of a military component is not its relative popularity in the body politic, but rather in its ability to deliver the intended results for the society it serves. Technology facilitates that end. Although many disparage the utility of high-technology weaponry, Americans need to appreciate that technology is, in fact, this country's asymmetric advantage. Recently, strategic theorist Colin Gray noted that "high technology is the American way in warfare. It has to be. A high technology society cannot possibly prepare for, or attempt to fight, its wars in any other than a technology-led manner."[96]

Overall, the "American way in warfare" has been the most successful in history. In a real way, the technology-intensive nature of airpower makes it eminently "American." To the extent it is abandoned or demeaned, the United States risks departing from a military approach that has the most promise to provide options to decision makers that, among other things, do not require placing masses of young Americans in harm's way. At the same time, air force leaders must be able to assist decision makers in their understanding of the military arts, as well as the science of weaponry. To do so effectively, they must comprehend fully, and be able to speak coherently about, the political, social, and economic contexts of twenty-first-century conflicts. In this area, the air force has much to learn from its sister services about how to produce leaders who are—and who appear to be—ready to provide such comprehensive advice.

It is imperative that the Air Force cultivate airmen—particularly at the senior level—with a stronger ability to advocate airpower. Secretary Michael Donley seemed to recognize this need when he observed that

> we need to be prepared to engage—and if necessary debate—the major issues facing our Air Force. Good stewardship demands developing a deep understanding of the macro-level trends affecting the Air Force. . . . As we do so, we will cultivate reasoned, carefully considered perspectives. We will be able to present these views not by digging in or staking out turf, but from a careful analysis and a seasoned appreciation of the many joint and national influences affecting today's strategic decision-making.[97]

In order to meet its challenges, the Air Force must be prepared to change those aspects of its culture that conflict with its large goals. It must also explore new means of reconciling the burdens of a highly demanding technical environment with the complex dynamics of human interactions, the mastery of which is proving so essential to success in twenty-first-century warfare.

5

Strategy, Counterinsurgency, and the Army

Robert Killebrew

As long as we try to employ our forces to "win" the insurgency [instead of to] help our friends, partners, and allies win *their* insurgency, we will focus on the wrong tasks. I believe we need a force that can operate across the spectrum—not every force can do everything and of course the challenge is balancing our force so that we can do what is required to defend our nation—from Foreign Internal Defense (which includes indirect, direct, and combat operations in support of a host nation) to major combat operations.

—Colonel David Maxwell, U.S. Army, April 2008[1]

Broadly speaking, modern warfare is fought either by regular forces arrayed on battlefields, or by "irregulars" who fight in the shadows and outside the rules. Although irregular warfare and counterinsurgency characterized life on the American frontier for nearly three hundred years, the modern-day experience of the United States with irregular warfare began on Friday, February 21, 1946, when Britain declared it could no longer bear the expense of supporting the government of Greece against a Communist insurgency. The Van Fleet mission to Greece, begun in 1948 to help the Greek government defeat the Soviet-backed insurgency, not only marked the emergence of the United States as the major anti-Communist power in Europe; it also showed, for the first time, what American political and military assistance could do for an embattled government. Moving rapidly and with a military logistics system still robust from World War II, General James Van Fleet moved advisors throughout the Greek army's command structure, stiffened the spine of field units, and opened a cornucopia of military hardware for the fielded forces. Aided by Tito's sealing of the Yugoslav borders to the insurgents, Greek forces took the offensive, and by 1950 the Greeks had won their counterinsurgency war, aided by American muscle.

The Greek insurgency established what might be called the "American Way of Counterinsurgency War": political support at home, diplomatic initiatives abroad to support friends and isolate the insurgents, and the stiffening of local security forces on the ground through American materiel aid and American advisors. Since Greece, this counterinsurgency strategy has generally succeeded, or is succeeding, as in El Salvador, Colombia, the Philippines, and lately in Iraq. Its notable failure was, of course, South Vietnam, where our inability to isolate the insurgency and our slowness in shifting the fighting to the South Vietnamese exhausted American patience. At this writing, Afghanistan remains a toss-up; despite a growing Afghan military capability, the U.S.-backed government of Hamid Karzai has not been able to diplomatically or militarily isolate the insurgency from bases in Pakistan's tribal territories.

The ability of the United States to execute successful counterinsurgency strategies will become more important as the world moves into a contentious twenty-first century. After the disappearance of the Soviet Union and Soviet-style communism, and at the beginning of the computer revolution, some theorists believed that advanced communications technologies would begin to erase national borders and the causes of interstate conflict. In books like Walter Wriston's *The Twilight of Sovereignty*, experts predicted the withering away of the state and the emergence of new, more benign governing structures.[2] What these books did not sufficiently recognize was that those same technologies were helping spread and magnify other destructive and even nihilistic ideologies that heretofore had had little worldwide reach.

The rise of groups espousing these ideologies—resulting most notably in the attacks on the World Trade Center and the Pentagon in September of 2001—led to a global reorientation of state power in the years afterward. On the one hand, internal security became an issue both here and overseas, and the powers of domestic and international police and intelligence organizations were strengthened and enlarged. The United States and its allies attacked the governments of Afghanistan and Iraq, involving Western powers more deeply and directly in the convoluted politics of the Middle East. Russia's recovery of Chechnya and resumption of its historic aggressive patterns of foreign policy, the rise of a powerful and all-but-nuclear Iran, and, above all, the emergence of China on the world stage as a voracious consumer of energy, all presage a resumption of state-on-state rivalry that would be familiar to any twentieth-century diplomat.

On the other hand, violent reaction to the U.S.-led invasions, as well as pre-existing ethnic and ideological conflicts and pervasive criminality, inflated the influence and capability of new insurgent groups, which were reinforced by new Internet technology that has helped nonstate groups to freely communicate, plan operations, and recruit. Support from rogue states has strengthened sub- or extranational organizations like Hezbollah and Hamas, lending credence to the view that, despite the temporary strengthening of state structures after 9/11, time is on the side of disintegrative forces. This trend looks very much like "fourth-generation warfare," a term from the late 1980s that describes a state of constant, if episodic, combat similar to the endless wars of premodern times, before states learned to control violence by grouping warriors into armies. It's possible that in the long term, stateless violence will eventually coalesce around political objectives that would be familiar to Mao or Che, but so far, insurgents' ability to operate globally gives us new models of irregular conflict. Irregular warfare in the twenty-first century is liable to be a mix of both familiar attempts to overthrow states, and more challenging, almost nihilistic forms of "uncontrolled combat" not motivated primarily, if at all, by an interest in governing or even in ending conflict. This nihilistic variant, far more difficult to counter than previous insurgencies, will be widely, even globally, dispersed, indifferent to political boundaries, and indiscriminate in violence, just as stateless warriors were indifferent in Europe's premodern period.

The two great currents in international affairs—the resumption of great-power competition and the rise of irregular warfare, including new-model insurgencies—will dominate military thinking for at least the first half of the new century. In practice, since military formations will be increasingly expensive, the high-tech forces designed for the most serious nation-on-nation contingencies will have to adapt on demand to the longer and more protracted irregular wars that are liable to be a staple of the international scene. But even though the forms of irregular warfare and insurgencies will have changed, American military strategy for conducting counterinsurgency warfare will remain much the same as it was in Van Fleet's day: U.S. leaders will attempt to maintain political support at home, conduct diplomatic initiatives to isolate insurgents and support friendly governments abroad, and support U.S. security assistance programs to our allies, either to fight ongoing insurgencies or to prevent them. Below I consider each part of this counterinsurgency triad (with a special focus on military programs) and show how each—political support at home, diplomacy overseas, and military assistance—is fundamental to the success of American security policy in the twenty-first century.

Political Support for Counterinsurgency

The America that supported Van Fleet's mission in 1948 and the America of today are vastly different, in public attitudes toward overseas commitments, in the legal and regulatory environments in which military strategy is executed, and in the public perception of the military instrument itself. Support for the Greek government came at the very beginning of the Cold War, at a time when the United States had just emerged from World War II; wartime channels of command and support were still largely in place; a great mass of war materiel was on hand; and American self-confidence had never been higher. The prolonged war in Vietnam, with over fifty-eight thousand dead, shattered the post-1945 consensus and led to a long chain of oversight "reforms" that made the provision of overseas military assistance more complex. Congressional criticism of U.S. participation in counterinsurgency—for example, in El Salvador—has increased markedly. Finally, the twenty-four-hour news cycle and the increasingly global nature of news broadcasting have meant that any event anywhere in the world, regardless of its true importance, might be discussed around American dinner tables and become fodder for U.S. political campaigns. Not for nothing do U.S. war college classes routinely opine that the U.S. center of gravity in counterinsurgency wars is American public opinion. The record shows, though, that a skillful president can parlay political capital into domestic support for counterinsurgency campaigns—provided U.S. casualties are kept low and operations appear to be succeeding.[3]

In addition to support in the executive branch, congressional support for military assistance programs is vital if these programs are to succeed. "Security force assistance" to foreign states almost always means materiel and training, both of which are overseen by a plethora of legislative and Department of State and Defense regulations. Many of these mechanisms sprouted up in the reaction against the Vietnam War. In the aftermath of Vietnam, and during the latter stages of the U.S.-Soviet confrontation, questions of military assistance to emerging states, "small wars," and irregular operations tended to be backwaters in strategic planning. As a consequence, little was done, or has been done, to fix the unwieldy tangle that military assistance programs have become.[4]

Additionally, because insurgency and counterinsurgency are waged on the political front as well as in the field, a mature, strong diplomatic corps is essential. In the U.S. system, ambassadors (also known as chiefs of mission) not only represent the United States to host governments; they also are responsible for the coordination and execution of U.S. programs in host countries that take place in the critical early stages of incipient insurgency. But ambassadors' capacity to shoulder this responsibility today has been severely curtailed. During the "strategic holiday" that followed the collapse of the Soviet Union, the State Department, the U.S. Agency for International Development (USAID), and other agencies were cut to the bone, personnel authorizations were chopped, and the diplomatic and political counterparts to military action, which are an essential part of any strategy of counterinsurgency and military assistance, were substantially weakened. While some progress is being made to reverse the cuts of the 1990s, there's still a long way to go before the State Department's personnel strength and funding are restored.

Finally, both political and military instruments must be closely aligned to ensure that military activities support diplomatic and political goals. Every authority from David Galula to the new army/marine field manual recognizes the need for close coordination of political and military goals in counterinsurgency. The question of who should be in charge, though, continues to elude a clear answer in American operations. Galula, one of the early writers on counterinsurgency (and still one of the best), is unequivocal:

> The inescapable conclusion is that the over-all responsibility should stay with the civilian power at every possible level. If there

is a shortage of trusted officials, nothing prevents filling the gap with military personnel serving in a civilian capacity. If the worst comes to the worst, the fiction, at least, should be preserved.[5]

But reflecting the particular American ambiguity between soldiers and statesmen, the army's counterinsurgency doctrine is less clear, stating only that

> ideally, a single counterinsurgent leader has authority over all government agencies involved in [counterinsurgency] operations. Usually, however, military commanders work to achieve unity of effort through liaison with a wide variety of nonmilitary agencies. The U.S. Ambassador and country team, along with senior [host nation] representatives, must be key players in higher level planning; similar connections are needed throughout the chain of command.[6]

The difference between Galula's precept that "the overall responsibility should stay with the civilian power at every possible level" and the field manual's contention that the ambassador and senior host nation representatives should be "key players" in planning is exactly the kind of ambiguity that should be cleared up before the United States enters a counterinsurgency campaign. While the army/marine field manual nods to the ideal condition of a "single counterinsurgent leader," the historical record indicates that national decision makers are less and less inclined to appoint one as the severity of the conflict, and its importance to the United States, increases—at exactly the time the war effort most needs a single authority at all levels, political, diplomatic, and military.

Clearly, when diplomatic and military authorities are at odds, any counterinsurgency mission is endangered; the most recent example is the split between Secretary of Defense Donald Rumsfeld and Secretary of State Colin Powell at the beginning of Operation Iraqi Freedom, and the havoc it caused in the field. Various presidents have attempted to adjudicate the lines of authority. President John F. Kennedy's distinction between military advisors and "forces in the field" is probably the most useful distinction to date; writing in 1961, Kennedy drew a clear distinction between the ambassador's authority over military assistance groups, which operated under normal

diplomatic authority, and fielded forces in wartime under a regional commander.[7] Whatever the final determination, a national-level decision as to
which agency of government will provide the single counterinsurgent leader
mentioned in doctrine is a vital and necessary step in preparing for successful counterinsurgency operations.

Diplomacy's Role in Counterinsurgency

The primary role of diplomacy in support of counterinsurgency is to strategically isolate insurgent movements and deny them sanctuaries in neighboring
countries. Successful modern insurgencies have invariably taken advantage of
a sanctuary state that has provided secure areas for recovery and training as
well as material aid; two examples from the mid-1980s are Nicaragua for the
El Salvadorian guerrillas and Pakistan for the anti-Soviet Mujahideen. Given
the increasing precision and lethality of modern weaponry, as well as quan-
tum increases in the ability of battlefield intelligence to detect and attack
insurgent hideouts, prolonged insurgent campaigns rely even more than in
years past on a sanctuary base beyond the reach of counterinsurgent forces.
Closing off access to those bases, or denying their use in other ways, should
be the objective of U.S. policy and should be pursued through whatever
means are both practical and in line with long-term U.S. goals. The broadest
range of options should be available to American diplomats to persuade
foreign governments to close off their borders to insurgents—favorable
trade agreements, U.S. support for local policy goals, foreign aid, or military
assistance programs for their own forces. In Pakistan today, and well below
the headlines, U.S. military assistance programs are helping the Pakistani
army grow its own capability to take on insurgents within Pakistan's border
areas with Afghanistan, and U.S. policy walks a tightrope with the government of Pakistan to eventually eliminate al Qaeda safe havens in Pakistan
along the Afghan border.

It bears repeating that the U.S. role in counterinsurgency will always
be to support the government or state under attack. As a consequence, to
ensure that insurgents are as politically isolated as possible, U.S. objectives
and strategies must be very closely aligned with those of the host country
and, radiating outward, with the attitudes of nearby states and with the

international community at large. Afghanistan is an excellent case in point; U.S. policy in support of the Afghan government must align not only with the objectives of the Karzai administration, but also with those of the government of Pakistan, the central Asian states neighboring Pakistan to the north, India, and, to an extent, Iran. Support for the United States in these cases is much more than just diplomatic courtesy: American supply lines run through neighboring states; American diplomats, soldiers, civilians, and investments in nearby states must be protected; and struggling governments receiving U.S. aid gain legitimacy in the eyes of their people when neighboring states ally with their cause.

Access to the broadest range of diplomatic options requires that U.S. diplomats work hand in hand with all branches of the U.S. government—most especially the Congress—to get approval for treaties and funding for counterinsurgency policies that may become enmeshed in domestic politics, particularly in election years. The historical record indicates, though, that bipartisan long-term support to allies threatened by insurgencies is feasible and has been successful in the past—witness our assistance to the government of Colombia. A U.S. administration that commits the United States to support a faltering ally must not only deploy diplomatic and military power; it must also achieve a bipartisan consensus within our own government so that forward diplomats and soldiers receive the support and backing they require to meet an insurgent challenge in the field.

Military Assistance and Country Teams

At the center of American contact with any foreign state is the U.S. country team. As a representative of the president, the ambassador represents all aspects of the U.S. relationship with the host country; he presides over an embassy staff headed by the deputy chief of mission and other State Department employees and officers. The embassy also contains representatives of other U.S. agencies, from the Central Intelligence Agency to the Agriculture Department, their exact composition and number depending on the host country and U.S. policies. Normally, an embassy staff includes military attachés—that is, military officers from all the services who represent their services to the host country and openly collect intelligence. Collectively, the embassy crowd is known as "the country team," a group that nominally operates under the supervision of the ambassador even as different agencies answer as well to higher authorities elsewhere. As former Ambassador Alexis Johnson said in 1961, "The Country Team does not appear in any formal constituting document. It is not defined in any NSC [National Security Council] directive. It is like the British Constitution, unwritten, yet nonetheless real."[8]

When military assistance begins to flow to a host country, the Department of Defense dispatches a military team to supervise disbursement of the aid and execute whatever function is associated with the aid—for example, maintenance training or tactical exercises to familiarize the host with the use of the new gear. Security assistance teams may be assigned to the host country on a temporary basis, or they may be permanently assigned under any of many titles agreed to by the host country; for simplicity here, teams that are permanently assigned are referred to as military groups, stationed in the host country and working under the U.S. ambassador. Members of military groups live in the country as part of the country team, working hand in hand with members of host country armed forces and building personal relationships to carry out the missions of both the host country and the United States.

At least, that's the way it's supposed to work. In fact, relationships between the country team and U.S. military forces have occasionally been spotty, as the aims of the military command system, operating through regional commanders, sometimes have been at odds with the State Department's objectives, working through the department's regional assistant secretaries and chiefs of mission. On the ground, though, the country team has been, and remains, the most effective means of achieving effective interagency operations, particularly at the low end of insurgency and irregular warfare.

Fighting Insurgencies in the Twenty-First Century

Not only America has changed since the Van Fleet mission; insurgency itself has changed. Classic insurgency pitted ill-equipped but ideologically committed guerrillas against the armies of a state; the objective was the overthrow of the state government and its replacement with another, more ideologically pure, state government. Although popular lore remembers insurgency success stories—Mao, Che, Ho—in fact, most insurgencies of the twentieth century were failures. The emerging insurgencies of the twenty-first century are far different in many ways from the politically motivated insurgencies of the last century. Political motivations are not so easily discerned, and armament has been modernized to such a degree that skirmishes with insurgents today may be occasionally difficult to distinguish from high-intensity warfare. The scholar Frank Hoffman and others have captured this change in a concept called "hybrid warfare." As Hoffman explains:

> Unlike in Maoist or compound wars, the purpose of the multimodal approach [in hybrid warfare] is not to facilitate the progression of the opposition force through phases nor is it to help set up a conventional force for decisive battle. Hybrid opponents, in contrast, . . . seek victory by the fusion of irregular tactics and the most lethal means available in order to attack and obtain their political objectives. . . . Criminal activity is used to . . . facilitate the disorder and disruption of the target nation.[9]

Hoffman's "hybrid warfare" accurately captures the nature of insurgencies in Iraq, Afghanistan, the Philippines, and Colombia; this type of fighting may become the norm for insurgent movements worldwide. Access to modern arms, terror attacks against the civilian population, criminal activity to support the insurgent force, and ideologically committed combatants have long characterized insurgent movements. What characterizes the new insurgencies is the lack of discernable "phases" of guerrilla movements (familiar to students of Mao), the lethality of attacks against civil populations, and the movements' ability to recruit and train, even worldwide, through the Internet. Further, the existence of states that sponsor insurgencies and terrorism—principally Iran—not only puts funding at the disposal of various anti-Western insurgent-cum-terror groups, but also (as in classic insurgencies) provides a strategic sanctuary for the leaders and financiers of insurgencies worldwide. These developments challenge the United States and its allies to refine the strategies of irregular warfare and counterinsurgency discussed above, mainly by applying them at the lower levels of warfare in support of struggling nations that will be the battlegrounds of irregular "hybrid" insurgencies in the new century.

Any discussion of counterinsurgency structures or methods must acknowledge the impact that U.S. military operations in Iraq and Afghanistan have had on defense planning. From the beginning of each conflict, the diplomatic component of U.S. strategy was either weak or wholly missing. In the case of Iraq, early dissonance between in-country political leadership and military commanders inhibited reaction to insurgency in its early stages. Combat in the two theaters since 2002 has caused intensive rethinking of military doctrines and techniques, reorientation of acquisition programs, and a shift in U.S. defense planning away from large-scale, high-intensity wars and toward the lower-intensity end of irregular war, of which counterinsurgency is only a part.

But the U.S. impulse to categorize warfare has run afoul of Hoffman's "hybrid war" concept, which more nearly fits present combat in Iraq, in particular, than does a neat compartmentalization of warfare into "irregular" and "conventional" modes. In fact, warfare in Iraq varies from counterinsurgency and nation-building activities to brief periods of high-intensity, combined-arms warfare, made more difficult because the United States and its allies are concurrently rebuilding Iraqi security forces and an Iraqi state with all its appendages. This is not an ideal counterinsurgency model. Many of the same conditions apply in Afghanistan, which—because of the Taliban safe havens in Pakistan—vividly illustrates the difficulty of prosecuting counterinsurgency operations when the enemy can shelter on the territory of a U.S. ally.

In their earlier stages, both Iraq and Afghanistan represented the worst-case counterinsurgency scenario: nonexistent host-nation civil authority, demobilized security forces, and insufficient U.S. and allied ground forces to fight a stubborn and inventive "hybrid" enemy. The direction and prosecution of conflict in both theaters have shown serious flaws, although in both theaters, slowly and over years of bloody warfare, civil authority is emerging, particularly in Iraq, along with gradual improvements in local security forces. The pace of change has been sufficiently slow, however, that political support within the United States and allied nations has receded. The United States will continue to have forces deployed to both theaters in one form or another for years to come.

Recommended Strategies for Twenty-First-Century Counterinsurgency

The Van Fleet mission was important not only because it helped Greece, but also because turning back the insurgents dealt a serious blow to the previously successful march of Communist aggression across Europe. Strategically, it prevented the USSR from extending its reach to the Mediterranean and helped persuade U.S. allies that the spread of communism could be contained. Likewise, outcomes of modern counter-terrorism campaigns will affect not only the locales where insurgents are confronted. They will also ultimately affect relations between states and global power balances. Contrary to the more heated arguments of counter-insurgency proponents, state-on-state competition has not gone away; high-intensity wars between states are still possible if power balances are upset or rogue states sense opportunities created by successful insurgencies. Further, even state-on-state conflicts may have "hybrid" qualities; warfare will have not only its high-intensity, force-on-force component but irregular dimensions that will be liable to spread across borders along ethnic or religious lines. Thus containing or defeating modern insurgencies in their earliest phases has strategic implications beyond the loss of an ally or a weak state.

Countering insurgency in its earliest stages is the coming shift in American strategy. Rather than committing American combat forces—which are seen as foreign troops, no matter how friendly the local government— when the situation is already dire, new strategies should call for assisting and strengthening local governments and security forces to *prevent* the outbreak of insurgencies in their territories, or, if insurgencies begin, to defeat them without direct U.S. involvement. How to structure and train U.S. forces for both these missions—direct combat in higher-intensity wars and advising and supporting our allies in the lower-end irregular wars of the future—is the issue. Five recommendations seem appropriate.

1. *Coordinate diplomatic and military action.* Existing U.S. diplomatic and military structures are generally sound for managing warfare at any end of the spectrum, from very low-level military assistance missions to emerging nations, through nuclear combat with peer competitors. The sticking point is developing mechanisms that permit concerted diplomatic and military action at lower levels of intensity—specifically counterinsurgency. There is little disagreement that the higher the intensity of combat, and the more immediate the threat to U.S. objectives or even survival, the more decisive the military voice should be. But in the deeply political irregular wars of the

future, political and diplomatic guidance should more directly oversee military assistance and action in the host country, as well as the actions of other government agencies in support of the host country. This guidance comes, and should continue to come, from the chief of mission, his deputy, and the U.S. country team.

Unfortunately, since post-Vietnam drawdowns and especially cutbacks in the 1980s and 1990s, many U.S. embassies today lack the staff, authority, and experience to serve in such a directive role. Spurred by the experiences in the Middle East, though, the State Department has begun an ambitious recruiting program to rebuild capabilities lost during the post–Cold War vacation from strategy; stronger, better-structured country teams are probable in the near future. This is an opportune moment for both the Defense Department and State Department to consider seriously concepts, mechanisms, and procedures that would enable better integration of military initiatives with diplomatic and political direction. For example, a presidential finding that a certain country (or region) is in a state of "preinsurgency" could lead to modified presidential directives to the ambassador and regional military commander that would enhance the authority of the ambassador relative to other U.S. governmental agencies represented in the country, including the military services. If the level of concern increased, the stage would be set for the creation of a military assistance group, the selection of certain key personnel, and other steps that have, in fact, been taken in the past on an ad hoc basis. Other ways for all agencies of government, including military, to assist the ambassador in countering incipient insurgencies should be examined and codified. The staffs of combatant commanders should, where possible, be expanded to include members of the diplomatic services as well as other agencies.[10] Hybrid warfare and the potential for irregular conflicts to strike directly at U.S. vital interests is fostering the integration of military and political direction in areas of conflict, and U.S. leaders should encourage the trend.

2. *Shift military culture to acknowledge the role of noncombatants and the primacy of the host country.* Two major cultural shifts must take place within the U.S. military, and in the ground forces in particular. The first, and simplest, will be recognizing that battlefields of the future are going to be populated, and that protecting and serving the host country populations will frequently be the object of military operations, rather than an irritating

impediment during combat. Clearly, in the Internet and videocam age, civilians have become an integral feature of military operations, and they will be more so in the hybrid warfare of the future. War will henceforth be conducted *among* the population, and, in the cases of counterinsurgency, *for* the population. While there have been other attempts to take civilian populations into account in military planning—the generation that fought Vietnam recognizes this paradigm—military planners and trainers have tended, during intervals of peace, to ignore concerns about fighters among the population. The impact of civilian populations on the battlefield will from now on be a central concern, like terrain or weather. The officers and noncommissioned officers (NCOs) coming of age in Iraq and Afghanistan recognize this, even if they sometimes find it uncomfortable. Balancing the aggressive tactics necessary for threat-focused combat with concern for the security of noncombatants must now become the norm for U.S. planning and training for land combat.

The other cultural shift, and one that marches alongside concern for the host country's civilian population, will be recognizing the primacy of the host country on future irregular battlefields. In almost every conceivable future conflict, the ultimate objective of U.S. forces will be to hand over the battle to forces of the host country and depart, or else provide combat support until the insurgency is ended. This is directly contrary to the blitzkreig-inspired (quick, decisive) victories foreseen in U.S. doctrine before the Iraq and Afghan wars. While U.S. forces may be—should be—capable of the rapid destruction of enemy forces, hard experience has shown that U.S. leadership is unlikely to withdraw forces without leaving behind some kind of effective local government and security force; this has been the case as far back as the post–World War II period, when ex-Wehrmacht soldiers were recruited for the West German Border Police. For America's armed forces, winning wars now includes turning authority over to local security forces and then supporting them. This implies that U.S. diplomatic and military objectives must be integrated with, and in some cases subordinate to, the political and military objectives of the host country as that country's security forces grow and become more effective through U.S. aid. The main objective of U.S. forces in the future, then, must be to support other armies, not to shoulder the entire burden of battle alone.

3. *Give chiefs of mission more authority.* The legal and regulatory structure of U.S. military and foreign aid assistance programs, ranging from foreign

military sales to outright gifts, should be modified to give the chief of mission more directive authority. This is a complex and difficult issue, involving as it does purchases of arms under multiyear procurements with impacts on the U.S. economy—the value of security assistance in the 2007 budget was over $62 billion—as well as funding that supports U.S. counterinsurgency efforts distributed by other government agencies, like USAID or the CIA. Three specific changes should be made. First, the chief of mission's embassy staff should be authorized and staffed to monitor funding for U.S. aid programs targeted for the host country. Second, if certain conditions are met—if, for example, a presidential "preinsurgency" determination has been made—the ambassador should be empowered to consolidate resources within the country team so that all U.S. programs in the country aim toward a common goal. While due allowance must be made for congressional strictures regarding the diversion of authorized funds, appropriate legislation should free the hands of the U.S. representative under certain conditions. Finally, and under the conditions specified above, the ambassador should be authorized to withhold various forms of U.S. assistance if he or she thinks it appropriate for the realization of national objectives.

Whatever the ambassador's authority is finally determined to be, there is little doubt that the role and influence of the ambassador should be enhanced in the early stages of U.S. counterinsurgency assistance to the host country. Both theory and experience argue for enlarging this role, as do a host of recent studies.[11] Effective interagency cooperation is not only more likely at the country-team level than in Washington; it is also more important there, where the proverbial rubber meets the road. Where chiefs of mission have achieved unity of effort in their missions in the past, it has often been because personalities meshed, and more by accident than by design. Clearly, happy accident is not a sufficient plan as the United States moves into an era of irregular and counterinsurgency challenges.

4. *Modify the military to address challenges of irregular warfare.* The military services themselves, and most particularly the army and Marine Corps, must modify their structuring and personnel planning to account for the new era of hybrid, irregular war. This is a considerable challenge. As warfare has gotten more complex, the skills required for regular armed forces to counter successfully threats across the spectrum of conflict have grown

exponentially; training an infantryman in, say, 1950 was much simpler than today, and the maintenance of basic skills took less time and was far less expensive than in modern times. Modern land forces in hybrid war must be capable of employing highly technical weapons and complex tactics in irregular wars that may change their nature village by village and block by block. This is a tremendous training challenge, exacerbated by continuing conflict in Iraq and Afghanistan, deployments to other theaters, the expectation of leaner budgets, and limited manpower. And from this force structure must also come manpower to fill military assistance groups and provide advisors to emerging states threatened by insurgencies.

The armies of emerging states expect and require the same kinds of advantages enjoyed by U.S. forces in their fight against insurgents—the Iraqis, for example, have repeatedly expressed their desire to replace their Soviet-style systems with American- or NATO-standard weaponry. The insurgents themselves will be well armed and will be using high-tech equipment either provided by a state sponsor or bought on the open market.[12] To be effective against well-armed enemies, and incidentally to allow the United States to achieve its own security goals in the region, friendly security forces must have access to first-line U.S. military technology and be trained in its use.

The military must recognize that in cases where initial counterinsurgency efforts are unsuccessful, and U.S. military personnel accompany host nation forces into the field, U.S. advisors and trainers will not only provide advice, but may well be the key to employment of other U.S. forces, ranging from air support to logistics, in support of host country security forces. The idea that U.S. forces could be employed piecemeal—for example, that an aviation brigade could be deployed to a counterinsurgency theater to support U.S. allies and American advisors without an accompanying all-arms structure—is not now a part of U.S. doctrine, but it was at one time. It must become so again. But such a doctrine—and, indeed, the successful employment of U.S. advisors and other forces in general—rests on three assumptions.

First, the intent of U.S. support must be to assist the host countries as described, and not simply to serve as an adjunct of unilateral employment of U.S. formations. The United States should not push local forces into a supporting or secondary role. The whole thrust of successful counterinsurgency warfare is to support and enhance the local government, not to make it an obvious dependent of the United States; we should see these countries as allies, not auxiliaries. This is obviously a key point in maintaining domestic political support for American involvement as well as support in the host country. Second, U.S. support must be a balanced program of military assistance that is responsive to the host country's needs, integrated into its forces, and accepted by its leadership, as managed for the United States by the chief of mission in consultation with the regional military commander. Third, U.S. military personnel must be qualified to execute advisor missions and be supported by an unencumbered logistics channel.

There is confusion in military circles about the nature of advisory duties and how they are discharged. An *advisor* is generally a military officer or NCO who is assigned to the host country for a regular tour of duty. Advisors are normally assigned to the military assistance group associated with the U.S. embassy. Like the country team, these groups are customized for the particular needs and requirements of the host country; they may be primarily focused on the reception and onward movement of military assistance in the form of foreign military sales, or they may be deeply involved in training the host country's army, air force, or navy. When authorized, assistance group members can take the field as advisors to the host country's security forces, either in training or active combat roles. These flexible and tailor-made groups are ideal organizations around which to build military responses to requests for assistance from friendly governments.

The other general form of direct military advice and assistance is through the deployment of mobile training teams. These teams are deployed to accomplish a specific task in the host country—build a bridge, train an artillery unit, introduce a new piece of equipment. Ideally, training teams are deployed in response to an ambassador's overall plan for the strategic development of U.S. relations with a host country and its armed forces, though sometimes additional teams may also be a part of a combatant command's training and exercising calendar. These teams are generally composed of small units, such as engineer companies, a rifle battalion, or a team of NCO experts on tank maintenance. As a rule, military planners tend to confuse training-team missions, which are of short duration, with advisory-type functions, which take place over a protracted period.

Finally, combined and joint exercises with host country armies fill gaps in local forces' training and are important and reassuring signals of American support. As a rule, nation-to-nation exercises are planned and coordinated at the regional command level, with the concurrence of the ambassador and of course the host government. Even under the press of the wars in Iraq and Afghanistan, the Pentagon has continued to support worldwide exercises as a means of "showing the flag," reassuring allies and helping host country security forces plan for combined operations, should the need ever arise.

The current weak point in this three-tiered concept of military assistance to allied nations—that is, security assistance, direct advisory and training missions, and the intervention of regular forces—is the selection and training of advisors for military assistance groups. This is a key deficiency, and one that must be remedied as the new strategic outreach to endangered nations comes on line under the "building partnership capacity" initiative. Military officers and NCOs should be selected for advisory duty because they are the best-qualified professionals in their military specialties, and not because they are of a certain ethnicity or possess a particular linguistic ability (though speaking the language is certainly a helpful qualification). To provide the most effective advisors possible to struggling states threatened by insurgency, the Department of Defense should make advisory duty a normal part of a standard military career, so that military professionals bring the latest military knowledge to their advisory assignments. The services should establish top-notch schools to prepare persons selected for advisory duty for that job; another approach would be to designate a service like the army as "executive agent" for creating a school for advisors like the now-defunct John F. Kennedy School for Military Assistance. A school for advisors should teach the best-qualified students the business of advising—advisor "lessons learned," the governmental system and culture of the destination host country, pedagogy, and enough language to get by initially. Once in country, advisors can continue language lessons, but the object should be to get the novice advisor to his or her destination while his or her combat skills are still fresh.

Requirements for military assistance groups will be hard to pin down from year to year. At this moment, no one knows how many of these groups or advisors will ultimately be required, though the next quadrennial defense review should begin this assessment. As time passes, and the new emphasis on outreach to threatened countries continues, the demand for advisors will expand; in the interim, doctrines, procedures, and the advisor school can be prepared and ready to meet the need.

5. *Expand the foreign population at U.S. military schools.* The numbers of foreign officers and NCOs attending U.S. military schools in the United States must be drastically increased, and the Pentagon should take steps to more actively encourage foreign countries to send their best officers to U.S. schools. In 2007, the army was hosting only seven thousand students from allied countries at various locations around the United States; foreign countries sending officers to school here are required by legislation to pay their expenses, which approach those charged by Ivy League colleges, and this makes attendance difficult for struggling states in Africa, for example. The Defense Department should explore ways to ease this financial burden, and the services should expand drastically the number of foreign officers in attendance, particularly at the senior levels. Attendance of U.S. officers at foreign schools should likewise be expanded, particularly at schools in areas of the world under threat. The commander of the U.S. Joint Forces Command, marine general Jim Mattis, has just recommended to the secretary of defense that numbers of foreign students at U.S. military educational institutions be drastically increased.

If U.S. strategy is shifting away from launching "expeditionary operations" to working cooperatively with foreign governments to turn back insurgencies before they become serious security threats, everything that can be done to build bridges between the U.S military and the future military leadership of our allies would seem to be worthwhile. Educating foreign military officers in U.S. schools has proven to be a very cost-effective way of spreading U.S. influence and building personal bonds between American officers and their foreign counterparts, who in many cases go on to be the heads of their services and even exercise political power in their governments.[13]

Conclusion

Whether U.S. forces deploy against the regular armies of other nation-states or U.S. military advisors disperse into low-key military assistance groups to help allies fight their own wars, "hybrid" insurgency warfare will characterize future conflicts for the foreseeable future. New technology, the Internet, ideological extremism, and the struggle of emerging nations to deal with surging populations, unemployment, crime, and corruption will define challenges beneath the more familiar competition between major powers. Yet the basic elements of American counterinsurgency strategy—political and diplomatic support, materiel and advisory assistance—will continue to underpin the strategy of support for emerging nations threatened with insurgencies. Most of the tools the United States needs in order to prevail in the wars of the twenty-first century are already here. If we act on the recommendations listed above, and if in particular we can both develop a system for unified direction of foreign military assistance in conditions of incipient insurgency and create a Department of Defense school for advisors, then the United States should be ready to win, and to help our friends win, the counterinsurgency campaigns of the twenty-first century.

Notes

Introduction

1. Harold Ickes, "We're Running Out of Oil!" *American Magazine*, December 1943; quoted in Daniel Yergin, *The Prize: The Epic Quest for Oil, Money & Power* (New York: Free Press, 1992), 395.

2. See CNN.com, "Transcript of Osama Bin Laden Videotape, December 13, 2001," http://archives.cnn.com/2001/US/12/13/tape.transcript/.

3. See Tom Donnelly, "Trying To Lose the War We're In," *Weekly Standard*, October 3, 2008, http://www.weeklystandard.com/weblogs/TWSFP/2008/10/trying_to_lose_the_war_were_in_1.asp.

Chapter 1: Domestic Politics and the Long War

1. See Peter D. Feaver, "Cold War II," *Weekly Standard*, October 1, 2001.

2. *The 2006 National Security Strategy of the United States* (Washington, D.C.: The White House), 2006, 9; available at http://georgewbush-whitehouse.archives.gov/nsc/nss/2006/.

3. See Douglas J. Feith, *War and Decision* (New York: Harper, 2008), 56.

4. George W. Bush, "Address to a Joint Session of Congress and the American People," September 20, 2001, http://www.whitehouse.gov/news/releases/2001/09/20010920-8.html.

5. Peter D. Feaver, "The Brits Are All Right," *Weekly Standard*, September 24, 2001.

6. Michael Howard, speech at the Royal United Services Institute, October 31, 2001.

7. "Foremost in our minds was the prospect that 9/11 might be succeeded by further large-scale attacks on the United States. That could permanently change the nature of American society, driving the government toward undesirable—even if necessary—protective measures." Feith, *War and Decision*, 10.

8. Paul O'Neill reports that dealing with the Iraq problem was at the top of the agenda of the first cabinet meeting he attended. See Ron Suskind, *The Price of Loyalty* (New York: Simon & Schuster, 2004), 72.

135

9. Colin Powell, "Reinvigorating U.S. Foreign Policy" (testimony before the House of Representatives Committee on International Relations, March 7, 2001), http://commdocs.house.gov/committees/intlrel/hfa71262.000/hfa71262_0f.htm.

10. Feith, *War and Decision*, 56.

11. See, for example, Andrew Bacevich, "Call It a Day," *Washington Post*, August 21, 2005; John Mueller, "What If We Leave?" *American Conservative*, February 26, 2007; and John Murtha, "Confessions of a 'Defeatocrat,'" *Washington Post*, October 15, 2006.

12. See, for example, Joseph Lieberman, "One Choice in Iraq," *Washington Post*, April 26, 2007; William Kristol, "Keep on Surgin'," *Weekly Standard*, July 23, 2007; and John McCain, "The War You're Not Reading About," *Washington Post*, April 7, 2007.

13. For a comprehensive analysis that concludes the public is willing to pay the costs of war provided that eventual success is in view, see Christopher Gelpi, Peter Feaver, and Jason Reifler, *Paying the Human Costs of War* (Princeton, NJ: Princeton University Press, 2009).

14. Frank Newport, "Americans Concerned About the Impact of Leaving Iraq," Gallup, March 14, 2008, http://www.gallup.com/poll/104977/Americans-Concerned-About-Impact-Leaving-Iraq.aspx.

15. Ron Paul, "Arguments Against a War in Iraq," Washington, D.C., September 4, 2002, http://www.ronpaul2008.com/articles/70/arguments-against-a-war-in-iraq/ .

16. For Obama's strategy, see Barack Obama, "The War We Need to Win" (speech, Woodrow Wilson Center for Scholars, Washington, D.C., August 1, 2007), http://www.barackobama.com/2007/08/01/remarks_of_senator_obama_the_w_1.php; the warning to Iran is from Hillary Clinton, quoted by Nazila Fathi, "Iran Protests Clinton's Words," *New York Times*, May 2, 2008, http://query.nytimes.com/gst/fullpage.html?res=9902EEDA1F30F931A35756C0A96E9C8B63&scp=1&sq=iran+protests+clinton+words&st=nyt.

17. "Problems and Priorities," PollingReport.com, January–June 2008, http://www.pollingreport.com/prioriti.htm.

18. Pew Research Center survey conducted by Princeton Survey Research Associates International, February 20–24, 2008, http://www.pollingreport.com/afghan.htm.

19. One Democratic friend considered partnering with me on a book in which we would write alternating chapters. He would outline the case against Republican abuse of national security for partisan purposes and I would outline the case against Democratic use of national security for partisan ends. Subsequent chapters would provide the rebuttals, and a conclusion would make a sensible appeal for post-partisanship dialogue. A publisher told us that there would be a market for either half of the book but not for both together!

20. "Democrats Critical of Bush's First 100 Days," CNN News, April 26, 2001, http://edition.cnn.com/TRANSCRIPTS/0104/26/se.01.html.

21. The tone is captured well in Condoleeza Rice, "Promoting the National Interest," *Foreign Affairs* 79, no. 1 (January/February 2000): 45–62.

22. See Jack Goldsmith, *The Terror Presidency* (New York: W. W. Norton, 2007), 141–76; and Bob Woodward, *Plan of Attack* (New York: Simon & Schuster, 2004), 61–63.

23. John Mearsheimer, "Guns Won't Win the Afghan War," *New York Times*, November 4, 2001,   http://query.nytimes.com/gst/fullpage.html?res=9404E4D61F30F937A 35752C1A9679C8B63.

24. Kevin Sullivan, "War Support Ebbs Worldwide; Sept. 11 Doesn't Justify Bombing, Many Say," *Washington Post*, November 7, 2001; Arie Farnam, "Bombings Hit Unintended Target: European Opinion," *Christian Science Monitor*, November 14, 2001, http://www. csmonitor.com/2001/1114/p7s2-woeu.html; and Carl Conetta, "Losing Hearts and Minds: World Public Opinion and post-9/11 US Security Policy," Project on Defense Alternatives, Briefing Memo #37, September 14, 2006, http://www.comw.org/ pda/0609bm37.html.

25. Steven Thomma, "Daschle, Democratic Leaders Sound Party's First Public Criticism of the War," *Knight Ridder Washington Bureau,* February 28, 2002.

26. *New York Times*, "The Limit of Power," January 31, 2002.

27. David M. Shribman, "From Change of Mind, Bush Gains Major Turning Point," *Boston Globe*, June 7, 2002.

28. David Firestone, "Threats and Responses: Domestic Security; Homeland Security Fight Returns to Fore," *New York Times*, October 16, 2002.

29. For this and other conspiracy theories, see 911truth.org.

30. Barack Obama, "Remarks of Illinois State Senator Barack Obama Against Going to War With Iraq," October 2, 2002, http://www.barackobama.com/2002/10/02/ remarks_of_illinois_state_sen.php.

31. James Carney, "General Karl Rove, Reporting for Duty," *Time*, September 29, 2002, http://www.time.com/time/nation/article/0,8599,356034,00.html.

32. See Scott McClellan, *What Happened: Inside the Bush White House and Washington's Culture of Deception* (New York: BBS, 2007), 66–71, 146.

33. "Newsmaker: Tom Daschle," *PBS Online Newshour*, September 17, 2002, http://www.pbs.org/newshour/bb/congress/july-dec02/daschle_9-17.html.

34. Obama, "Remarks Against Going to War With Iraq."

35. See Todd S. Purdum, "The U.S. Case against Iraq: Counting Up the Reasons," *New York Times*, October 1, 2002.

36. Mike Allen and Jim VandeHei, "Bush: Unity Soon on Iraq; Democrats Seek More Negotiation on War Resolution," *Washington Post*, September 27, 2002.

37. E. J. Dionne Jr., "Bush is Boxing the Democrats on Iraq," *Boston Globe*, September 21, 2002.

38. Frank Cannon & Chuck Donovan, "The Seriousness Gap," *Weekly Standard*, November 18, 2002, http://www.weeklystandard.com/Content/Public/Articles/000/ 000/001/898oemoa.asp; Jeffrey Gettleman, "The 2002 Elections: Georgia," *New York Times*, November 6, 2002, http://query.nytimes.com/gst/fullpage.html?res=9402E1D E113EF935A35752C1A9649C8B63.

39. Rich Lowry, "Max Cleland, Liberal Victim," *National Review*, February 20, 2004, http://www.nationalreview.com/lowry/lowry200402200857.asp.

40. Carla Marinucci and John Wildermuth, "The Candidates: Bush and Kerry Declare America's Resolve—Then Get Back to Politics," *San Francisco Chronicle*, October 30,

2004, http://www.sfgate.com/cgi-bin/article.cgi?f=/c/a/2004/10/30/CAMPAIGN.TMP; Elisabeth Bumiller and David M. Halbfinger, "Bush and Kerry Camps Clash on bin Laden Tape," *New York Times*, October 31, 2004; and "Second-Guessing Actions in Afghanistan," *Washington Post*, October 22, 2004.

41. Richard Clarke, *Against All Enemies: Inside America's War on Terror* (New York: Free Press, 2004).

42. Laura Blumenfeld, "Former Aide Takes Aim at War on Terror," *Washington Post*, June 16, 2003.

43. Dan Eggen and Steve Coll, "9/11 Panel Calls for Major Changes," *Washington Post*, July 18, 2004; and Suzanne Goldenberg, "Bush Ignored Warnings on Iraq Insurgency Threat Before Invasion," *Guardian*, September 29, 2004, http://www.guardian.co.uk/world/2004/sep/29/iraq.usa.

44. Mike Glover, "Kerry's 'Band of Brothers' Bolsters Campaign," *AP Worldstream*, January 28, 2004.

45. Michael Dobbs, "Swift Boat Accounts Incomplete," *Washington Post*, August 22, 2004, A.1.

46. Michael Kinsley, "To Swift-Boat or Not," *Time*, June 12, 2008, http://www.time.com/time/magazine/article/0,9171,1813974,00.html.

47. Mackubin Thomas Owens, "Seared in My Memory," *National Review*, September 20, 2004, http://www.nationalreview.com/script/printpage.p?ref=/owens/owens200409200858.asp.

48. See "New Questions on Bush Guard Duty," CBS News, September 20, 2004 http://www.cbsnews.com/stories/2004/09/08/60II/main641984.shtml; and Evan Thomas, "The Vets Attack," *Newsweek*, November 15, 2004.

49. "October is Time for Election 'Surprise,'" Associated Press, October 3, 2004, http://www.foxnews.com/story/0,2933,134315,00.html.

50. Maggie Michael, "Bin Ladin, in Statement to U.S. People, Says He Ordered September 11 Attacks," Associated Press, October 29, 2004.

51. See John Wildermuth and Carla Marinucci, "Two Days to Go: Both Camps Seek Edge from bin Laden Tape," *San Francisco Chronicle*, October 31, 2004, http://www.sfgate.com/cgi-bin/article.cgi?file=/c/a/2004/10/31/MNG5O9JIJM1.DTL&type=printable; and Michael Kinsley, "Osama's Candidate," *Washington Post*, September 26, 2004, B7.

52. Jim Michaels, "U.S., Iraqi Forces Gear Up to Retake Fallujah," *USA Today*, October 19, 2001, http://www.usatoday.com/news/world/iraq/2004-10-19-fallujah_x.htm.

53. Sheryl Gay Stolberg and Mark Mezzetti, "Democrats Push for Troop Cuts Within Months," *New York Times*, November 13, 2006, http://www.nytimes.com/2006/11/13/washington/13military.html?fta=y.

54. George W. Bush, "President's Address to the Nation," Office of the Press Secretary, January 10, 2007, http://www.whitehouse.gov/news/releases/2007/01/20070110-7.html.

55. "Nancy Pelosi Interview on 'The Charlie Rose Show,'" *International Herald Tribune*, June 28, 2007, http://www.iht.com/articles/2007/06/28/america/28rose-pelosi.php?page=1.

56. Leslie Gelb, cited in Michael Abramowitz and Karen DeYoung, "Next President Will Discover if U.S. Footprint Stabilizes Iraq," *Washington Post*, April 10, 2008, http://www.washingtonpost.com/wp-dyn/content/article/2008/04/09/AR2008040903701_pf.html.

57. See Michael Crowley, "Barack in Iraq," *New Republic*, May 7, 2008, http://www.tnr.com/politics/story.html?id=6001af15-399f-4b11-b7fb-6f52baca6bcc; and Thomas Friedman, "Whether Obama or McCain, Three Realities Will Confront New U.S. President," *New York Times*, June 19, 2008, http://www.stltoday.com/stltoday/news/stories.nsf/editorialcommentary/story/ADBEB4499C624C728625746D006C001E?OpenDocument.

58. Obama, "Remarks Against Going to War with Iraq."

59. John Bresnahan, "House Democrats' New Strategy: Force Slow End to War," *The Politico*, February 13, 2007, http://www.politico.com/news/stories/0207/2751.html.

60. "Senator Reid on Iraq: 'This War is Lost,'" CBS News, Washington, April 20, 2007, http://www.cbsnews.com/stories/2007/04/20/politics/main2709229.shtml.

61. Peter D. Feaver, "MoveOn's McCarthy Moment," *Boston Globe*, September 11, 2007.

62. Senator Carl Levin said, "Regardless of one's view of the wisdom of the policy that took us to Iraq in the first place and has kept us there over five years, we owe Petraeus and Odierno a debt of gratitude. And regardless how long the administration may choose to remain engaged in the strife in that country, our troops are better off with the leadership these two distinguished soldiers provide." Cited in David Stout, "2 Generals Optimistic About Cut in Iraqi Troops," *International Herald Tribune*, May 23, 2008.

63. Carl Hulse and Jeff Zeleny, "Bush and Cheney Chide Democrats on Iraq Deadline," *New York Times*, April 25, 2007, http://www.nytimes.com/2007/04/25/washington/25cong.html. Peter Baker, "For Bush, Advances But Not Approval," *Washington Post*, November 19, 2007; Mario Loyola, "(D) Is for Defeatist," National Review Online, April 4, 2007, http://www.cbsnews.com/stories/2007/04/04/opinion/main2645852.shtml.

64. Gail Russell Chaddock, "On Iraq War, Senate Leader Harry Reid in Cross Hairs," *Christian Science Monitor*, April 27, 2007, http://www.csmonitor.com/2007/0427/p01s02-uspo.html?page=1.

65. Fred Barnes, "Patriotism Paranoia," *Weekly Standard*, April 14, 2008.

66. Mike Glover, "Obama Stops Wearing Flag Pin," Associated Press, October 5, 2007, http://www.washingtonpost.com/wp-dyn/content/article/2007/10/05/AR2007100501027.html.

67. Senator Bob Graham, quoted by Fred Barnes, "The Last Refuge of the Democrats," *Weekly Standard*, December 15, 2003, http://www.weeklystandard.com/Content/Public/Articles/000/000/003/462ajcmr.asp.

68. Radha Iyengar and Jonathan Monten, "Is There an 'Emboldenment' Effect? Evidence from the Insurgency in Iraq," May 2008, http://people.rwj.harvard.edu/~riyengar/insurgency.pdf.

69. This is the aspect of the Valerie Plame affair that has received comparatively little attention in the otherwise exhaustive commentary on the subject. The Fitzgerald

investigation had a chilling effect on the administration's willingness to vigorously defend itself against what it considered to be baseless or false charges. As one commentator has observed, "In part because the Plame affair succeeded in criminalizing or semi-criminalizing effective defenders of the Iraq invasion, in part because the weapons of mass destruction were missing—perhaps even in part because the partisan polarization that predated 9/11 was never destined to go away for long—the administration lost its voice." Jeffrey Bell, "The Politics of a Failed Presidency," *Weekly Standard*, March 17, 2008, http://www.weeklystandard.com/Content/Public/Articles/000/000/014/857bstgi.asp. It is also striking how many of the alleged misdeeds in Congressman Conyers' long bill of particulars against the administration were nothing more than attempts by the administration to explain itself in response to attacks on its national security policies. See John C. Conyers, Jr., *The Constitution in Crisis* (New York: Skyhorse Publishing, 2007).

70. Bryan Burrough, Evgenia Peretz, David Rose, and David Wise, "The Path to War," *Vanity Fair*, May 2004, 228; "In Iraq Crisis, Networks are Megaphones for Official Views," FAIR, March 18, 2003, http://www.fair.org/index.php?page=1628; Russell Mokhiber and Robert Weissman, "The Unbalanced Hawks at the *Washington Post*," *Progressive*, March 4, 2003, http://www.commondreams.org/views03/0304-07.htm; and Chaim Kaufmann, "Threat Inflation and the Failure of the Marketplace of Ideas: The Selling of the Iraq War," *International Security* 29, no. 1 (Summer 2004): 5–48.

71. Referencing the period in the run-up to the war when he was a more junior official, McClellan claimed that the media was too soft on the administration. See McClellan, *What Happened*, 124–26.

72. James Risen and Eric Lichtblau, "Bush Lets U.S. Spy on Callers Without Courts," *New York Times*, December 16, 2005, http://www.nytimes.com/2005/12/16/politics/16program.html?th=&emc=th&pagewanted=all; Josh Meyer and Greg Miller, "U.S. Secretly Tracks World's Money Web," *San Francisco Chronicle*, June 23, 2006, http://www.sfgate.com/cgi-bin/article.cgi?file=/c/a/2006/06/23/MNG6UJJ9S01.DTL; and Leslie Cauley, "NSA Has Massive Database of Americans' Phone Calls," *USA Today*, May 11, 2006, http://www.usatoday.com/news/washington/2006-05-10-nsa_x.htm.

73. Peter Baker, "Surveillance Disclosure Denounced," *Washington Post*, June 27, 2006, http://www.washingtonpost.com/wp-dyn/content/article/2006/06/26/AR2006062600563_pf.html.

74. Charles Johnson, "Reuters Doctoring Photos from Beirut?" *Little Green Footballs*, August 5, 2006, http://littlegreenfootballs.com/weblog/?entry=21956&only.

75. "Power Line Wins, CBS News Loses," Power Line, September 9, 2004, http://www.powerlineblog.com/archives/2004/09/.

76. Mark Memmot, "Scoops and Skepticism: How the Story Unfolded," *USA Today*, September 21, 2004.

77. The various surveys and demographic data describing this are collected at "Media Bias Basics," Media Research Center, http://www.mediaresearch.org/biasbasics/biasbasics.asp.

78. Tim Groseclose and Jeffrey Milyo, "A Measure of Media Bias," *Quarterly Journal of Economics* 120, no. 4 (2005): 1191–1237.

79. During one debate, she joked (referring to a skit that showed reporters fawning on Obama): "If you saw 'Saturday Night Live' last Saturday, maybe we should ask Barack if he's comfortable and get him another pillow." Cited in Glenn Thrush, "Clinton Accuses Media of pro-Obama Bias at Debate," *Newsday*, February 26, 2008, http://www.newsday.com/news/nationworld/ny-usdeba0227,0,6808879.story. For an example of what she was complaining about, see the fawningly pro-Obama story by Richard Wolffe, Holly Bailey, and Evan Thomas, "Obama's 'Bubba Gap,'" *Newsweek*, May 5, 2008, http://www.newsweek.com/id/134398.

80. Scott Shane, "Bush's Iraq Speech Echoes a New Voice," *International Herald Tribune*, December 4, 2005, http://www.iht.com/articles/2005/12/04/news/diplo.php.

81. David E. Sanger, "Bush Gives Plan for Iraq Victory and Withdrawal," *New York Times*, December 1, 2005, http://www.nytimes.com/2005/12/01/politics/01bush.html?fta=y&oref=login; Brian Knowlton, "Criticizing Bush's New Iraq Strategy, Democrats Call for 'Real Plan,'" *International Herald Tribune*, November 30, 2005, http://www.iht.com/articles/2005/11/30/news/react.php.

82. In his press conference, Murtha stated, "Our military's done everything that has been asked of them. The U.S. cannot accomplish anything further in Iraq militarily. It's time to bring the troops home." See "Representative Murtha Holds a News Conference on the War in Iraq," *Washington Post*, November 17, 2005, http://www.washingtonpost.com/wp-dyn/content/article/2005/11/17/AR2005111700982.html.

83. Harold Meyerson, "Exit Strategy in Search of a Party," *Washington Post*, November 23, 2005, http://www.washingtonpost.com/wp-dyn/content/article/2005/11/22/AR2005112201356_pf.html.

84. David E. Sanger, "Spell 'No Comment' for Us, Please," *New York Times*, April 23, 2006; Tim Rutton, "'What Happened' by Scott McClellan," *Los Angeles Times*, May 20, 2008, http://www.latimes.com/features/books/la-et-rutten30-2008may30,0,1639634.story; and Keith Olbermann, "McClellan Stands by Barnburner Book," MSNBC, May 29, 2008, http://www.msnbc.msn.com/id/24883051/.

85. Peter D. Feaver, "Why We Went Into Iraq," *Weekly Standard*, March 24, 2008, http://www.weeklystandard.com/Content/Public/Articles/000/000/014/884qfzox.asp; and Douglas Feith, "How Bush Sold the War," *Wall Street Journal*, May 27, 2008.

86. Jennifer Medina, "War Veterans Lend Support to Lieberman in TV Ads," *New York Times*, September 2, 2006, http://www.nytimes.com/2006/09/02/nyregion/00lieberman.html?scp=10&sq=vets+for+freedom&st=nyt; Michael Crowley, "Can Lobbyists Stop the War?" *New York Times Magazine*, September 9, 2007; George Packer, "The Fall of Conservatism," *New Yorker*, May 26, 2008, http://www.newyorker.com/reporting/2008/05/26/080526fa_fact_packer; and David Horowitz and Jacob Heilbrunn, "How Important is the Left's Influence on American Politics?" *FrontPage Magazine*, May 6, 2005, http://www.frontpagemag.com/Articles/Read.aspx?GUID=D92142B7-4AA0-4FB6-977C-0DB27F2172B5.

87. This myth is especially resilient. Thus, the initial coverage of a massive Institute for Defense Analyses study of Iraqi archives documenting those linkages actually misreported the study's basic thrust. The reporter quoted out of context the statement that no "smoking gun" operational collaboration with al Qaeda was uncovered, ignoring the extensive coverage of links that essentially proved the administration's line. See Institute for Defense Analyses, "Iraqi Perspectives Project," Federation of American Scientists, November 2007, http://www.fas.org/irp/eprint/iraqi/index.html. See also Warren Strobel, "Exhaustive Review Finds No Link Between Saddam and al Qaeda," *McClatchy Newspapers*, March 10, 2008, http://www.mcclatchydc.com/227/story/29959.html.

88. See Peter Feaver, "Anatomy of the Surge," *Commentary*, April 2008, 24–28.

89. It is not entirely absent. Some in the media criticized Senator Obama for willfully distorting Senator McCain's "hundred year" comments about troop deployments in Iraq. See, for example, Michael Dobbs, "McCain's '100-Year War," *Washington Post*, March 17, 2008, http://blog.washingtonpost.com/fact-checker/2008/04/mccains_100year_war.html. However, even after the prevarication was exposed, the Obama campaign continued to use the misleading attack line with impunity.

Chapter 2: Renegotiating the Civil-Military Bargain after 9/11

1. I am indebted to Andrew Bacevich for this formulation of the problem in a comment on an early version of my proposal for a book tentatively titled *Sword of Republican Empire: A History of U.S. Civil-Military Relations*.

2. On these topics, see, for example, Charles C. Moskos, John Allen Williams, and David R. Segal, eds., *The Postmodern Military: Armed Forces After the Cold War* (New York: Oxford University Press, 2000); Laura L. Miller and John Allen Williams, "Do Military Policies on Gender and Sexuality Undermine Combat Effectiveness?" in *Soldiers and Civilians: The Civil-Military Gap and American National Security*, ed. Peter D. Feaver and Richard H. Kohn (Cambridge, MA: MIT Press, 2001), 361–402; and John Allen Williams, "The Military and Society Beyond the Postmodern Era," *Orbis* 52, no. 2 (Spring 2008): 199–216.

3. See Risa Brooks, *Shaping Strategy: The Civil-Military Politics of Strategic Assessment* (Princeton: Princeton University Press, 2008); and Michael Desch, *Power and Military Effectiveness: The Fallacy of Democratic Triumphalism* (Baltimore: Johns Hopkins University Press, 2008).

4. Richard H. Kohn, "The Erosion of Civilian Control of the Military in the United States Today," *Naval War College Review* 50, no. 3 (Summer 2002): 10.

5. See Frank G. Hoffman, "Dereliction of Duty Redux?: Post-Iraq Civil-Military Relations," *Orbis* 52, no. 2 (Spring 2008): 217–35. and Bob Woodward, *The War Within: A Secret White House History, 2006–2008* (New York: Simon and Schuster, 2008). As discussed below, Woodward reveals that many senior military leaders—most notably General George Casey, the overall commander in Iraq (now army chief of staff) and

Admiral William "Fox" Fallon—not only did not buy into the surge but also actively resisted the president's policy in Iraq.

6. See Greg Newbold, "Why Iraq Was a Mistake," *Time*, April 17, 2006; and David S. Cloud and Eric Schmitt, "More Retired Generals Call for Rumsfeld Resignation," *New York Times*, April 14, 2006, A1. For a concise but useful summary of the episode, see David Margolick, "The Night of the Generals," *Vanity Fair*, March 13, 2007, www.vanityfair.com/politics/features/2007/04/iraqgenerals200704?printable=true&c.

7. The remarks were made during an interview on *60 Minutes*, May 21, 2004, http://www.cbsnews.com/stories/2004/05/21/60minutes/main618896.shtml.

8. Quoted in Paul Eaton, "A Top-Down Review for the Pentagon," *New York Times*, March 19, 2006 http://www.nytimes.com/2006/03/19/opinion/19eaton.html?_r=1.

9. Matthew Moten, "A Broken Dialogue: Rumsfeld, Shinseki, and Civil-Military Tensions," in Suzanne C. Nielsen and Don M. Snider, eds., *American Civil-Military Relations: The Soldier and the State in a New Era* (Baltimore: Johns Hopkins University Press, 2009), 42–71.

10. Brooks, *Shaping Strategy*, 226–35; Mackubin Thomas Owens, "Reshaping Tilted Against the Army," *Washington Times*, November 24, 2002. For a critique of the ideas underpinning "transformation," see Owens, "Technology, the RMA, and Future War," *Strategic Review* 26, no. 2 (Spring 1998): 63–70.

11. Academics have not been immune to such animosity. See, for instance, Dale Herspring, *Rumsfeld's Wars: The Arrogance of Power* (Lawrence, KA: University Press of Kansas, 2008). For a contrary assessment, see Robert Kaplan, "What Rumsfeld Got Right: How Donald Rumsfeld Remade the U.S. Military for a More Uncertain World," *Atlantic Monthly*, July/August 2008, http://www.theatlantic.com/doc/200807/rumsfeld.

12. H. R. McMaster, *Dereliction of Duty: Lyndon Johnson, Robert McNamara, the Joint Chiefs of Staff, and the Lies That Led to Vietnam* (New York: Harper Collins, 1997).

13. Ole Holsti, "Of Chasms and Convergences: Attitudes and Beliefs of Civilians and Military Elites at the Start of a New Millennium," in *Soldiers and Civilians: The Civil-Military Gap and American National Security*, ed. Peter D. Feaver and Richard H. Kohn (Cambridge, MA: MIT Press, 2001), 84, 489, and tables 1.27, 1.28.

14. Eliot A. Cohen, *Supreme Command: Soldiers, Statesmen, and Leadership in Wartime* (New York: Free Press, 2002).

15. See Lewis Sorley, *A Better War: The Unexamined Victories and Final Tragedy of America's Last Years in Vietnam* (New York: HBJ/Harvest Books, 2000).

16. See Michael Gordon and Bernard Trainor, *The Generals' War: The Inside Story of the Conflict in the Gulf* (Boston: Little Brown and Company, 1995).

17. David Ignatius, "Rumsfeld and the Generals," *Washington Post*, March 30, 2005, A15, http://www.washingtonpost.com/wp-dyn/articles/A11309-2005Mar29.html.

18. For instance, see Cragg Hines, "Clinton's Vow to Lift Gay Ban is Reaffirmed," *Houston Chronicle*, November 12, 1992, A1; Barton Gellman, "Clinton Says He'll 'Consult' on Allowing Gays in Military," *Washington Post*, November 13, 1992, A1; U.S.

Department of Defense, Office of the Inspector General, *The Tailhook Report: The Official Inquiry into the Events of Tailhook '91* (New York: St. Martin's, 1993); William McMichael, *The Mother of All Hooks* (New Brunswick, NJ: Transaction Publishers, 1997); Elaine Sciolino, "B-52 Pilot Requests Discharge That is Honorable," *New York Times*, May 18, 1997, A1; Bradley Graham, "Army Leaders Feared Aberdeen Coverup Allegations," *Washington Post*, November 11, 1996, A1.

19. See Peter Feaver, *Armed Servants: Agency, Oversight, and Civil-Military Relations* (Cambridge, MA: Harvard University Press, 2003).

20. Colin Powell, "Why Generals Get Nervous," *New York Times*, October 8, 1992.

21. Colin Powell, "U.S. Forces: Challenges Ahead," *Foreign Affairs*, Winter 1992–93, 32–42.

22. See, for example, Richard Kohn, "Out of Control: The Crisis in Civil-Military Relations," *National Interest* 35 (Spring 1994): 3–17; and Russell F. Weigley, "The American Military and the Principle of Civilian Control from McClellan to Powell," *Journal of Military History* 57, no. 5 (October 1993): 28–30.

23. See, for example, Richard A. Serrano and Art Pine, "Many in Military Angry Over Clinton's Policies," *Los Angeles Times*, October 19, 1993, 1.

24. Warren Strobel, "This Time Clinton is Set to Heed Advice from Military," *Washington Times*, December 1, 1995, 1.

25. Kohn, "Erosion of Civilian Control," 21, n. 5. Cf. Eric Schmitt, "Joint Chiefs Accuse Congress of Weakening U.S. Defense," *New York Times*, September 30, 1998, 1; and Elaine Grossman, "Congressional Aide Finds Spending on 'Core Readiness' in Decline," *Inside the Pentagon*, June 28, 2001, 1.

26. See Michael Gordon and Bernard Trainor, *Cobra II: The Inside Story of the Invasion and Occupation of Iraq* (New York: Pantheon, 2006), 117.

27. Thom Shanker, "2 Leaders Ousted From Air Force in Atomic Errors," *New York Times*, June 6, 2008, http://www.nytimes.com/2008/06/06/washington/06military.html?_r=1&adxnnl=1&ref=todayspaper&adxnnlx=1212735795-6qfVDvbLA5+MI1/c0v7/bg&oref=slogin.

28. "Gates Approves New Defense Strategy Over Objections of Service Chiefs," *The Insider from Inside Defense*, June 12, 2008, http://insidedefense.com/secure/insider_display.asp?f=defense_2002.ask&docid=6122008_june12d.

29. See Woodward, *War Within*.

30. Cohen, *Supreme Command*, 4.

31. Samuel Huntington, *The Soldier and the State: The Theory and Politics of Civil-Military Relations* (Cambridge, MA: Belknap Press of Harvard University Press, 1957).

32. Ibid., 83.

33. Ibid., 84.

34. Michael Desch, "Bush and the Generals," *Foreign Affairs* 86, no. 3 (May-June 2007), http://www.foreignaffairs.org/20070501faessay86309/michael-c-desch/bush-and-the-generals.html. For replies to Desch, see Richard B. Myers and Richard H. Kohn; Mackubin Thomas Owens; and Lawrence Korb, "Salute and Disobey?" *Foreign Affairs* 86, no. 5 (September-October 2007): 147–56, http://www.foreignaffairs.org/20070901

faresponse86511/richard-b-myers-richard-h-kohn-mackubin-thomas-owens-lawrence-j-korb-michael-c-desch/salute-and-disobey.html.

35. Cohen, *Supreme Command*, 1–15.

36. Thomas E. Ricks, "Army Historian Cites Lack of Postwar Plan: Major Calls Effort in Iraq 'Mediocre,'" *Washington Post*, December 25, 2004, A01, http://www.washingtonpost.com/wp-dyn/articles/A24891-2004Dec24.html. Passages from Wilson's report quoted here are taken from the *Washington Post* article by Ricks.

37. On Rumsfeld and the plans for the Iraq War, see Gordon and Trainor, *Cobra II*; and Thomas Ricks, *Fiasco: The American Military Adventure in Iraq* (New York: Penguin, 2006).

38. John Garofano, "Effective Advice in Decisions for War: Beyond Objective Control," *Orbis* 52, no. 2 (Spring 2008): 253.

39. Ricks, *Fiasco*, 79–80.

40. Ibid., 97.

41. Garofano, "Effective Advice," 254.

42. Samuel P. Huntington, "National Policy and the Transoceanic Navy," *Proceedings* 80, no. 5 (May 1954): 483.

43. Carl H. Builder, *The Masks of War: American Military Styles in Strategy and Analysis* (Baltimore: Johns Hopkins University Press, 1989).

44. Ibid., 39.

45. For example, see Brian MacAllister Linn, *The Philippine War, 1899–1902* (Lawrence, KA: University Press of Kansas, 2000); Max Boot, *Savage Wars of Peace: Small Wars and the Rise of American Power* (New York: Basic Books, 2002); John Gates, "Indians and Insurrectos: The U.S. Army's Experience with Insurgency," *Parameters* 13 (March 1983): 59–68.

46. See Stephen Ambrose, *Upton and the Army* (Baton Rouge: Louisiana State University Press, 1964).

47. See Emory Upton, *The Military Policy of the United States* (Washington, DC: Government Printing Office, 1904).

48. For an excellent account of this argument, see Sorley, *A Better War*.

49. Lieutenant Colonel Paul Yingling, "A Failure in Generalship," *Armed Force Journal*, May 2007, http://www.armedforcesjournal.com/2007/05/2635198.

50. See Ann Scott Tyson, "Army's Next Crop of Generals Forged in Counterinsurgency," *Washington Post*, May 15, 2008, A4; and Tyson, "Petraeus Helping to Pick New Generals," *Washington Post*, November 17, 2007, A1.

51. Andrew J. Bacevich, "The Petraeus Doctrine," *Atlantic*, October 2008, http://www.theatlantic.com/doc/200810/petraeus-doctrine; Michael Horowitz, "The Future of War and American Strategy," *Orbis* 53, no. 2 (Spring 2009): 300–318.

52. Blue Ribbon Defense Panel, *Report to the President and the Secretary of Defense on the Department of Defense* (Washington, D.C.: Department of Defense, 1970), 50.

53. Quoted in Tim Reid, "Admiral William Fallon quits over Iran policy," Times Online, March 12, 2008, http://www.timesonline.co.uk/tol/news/world/us_and_americas/article3534102.ece.

54. Thomas P. M. Barnett, "The Man Between War and Peace," *Esquire*, April 23, 2008, http://www.esquire.com/features/fox-fallon. Subsequent quotations of Barnett are from this article.

55. Cited in ibid.

56. "Fallon: Iran Strike 'Strategic Mistake,'" Press TV, November 12, 2007, http://www.presstv.ir/detail.aspx?id=30790.

57. For a sympathetic portrait of Fallon, see Elaine Sciolino, "Push for New Direction Leads to Sudden Dead End for a 40-Year Naval Career," *New York Times*, May 31, 2008, 7.

58. The firing of Richardson as commander of the U.S. Pacific Fleet makes clear that even a private disagreement can cause a commander in chief to lose confidence in his subordinates. When President Roosevelt decided to move the U.S. Pacific Fleet from California to Pearl Harbor during the summer of 1940 in an effort to deter Japanese expansionism, Richardson objected, arguing that the move was provocative and could precipitate a war with Japan. The president fired him and replaced him with Rear Admiral Husband E. Kimmel. As Admiral Harold Stark, the chief of naval operations, wrote to Kimmel after the affair, "This, of course, is White House prerogative and responsibility, and believe me, it is used these days." Cited in Eric Larrabee, *Commander in Chief: Franklin Delano Roosevelt, His Lieutenants, and Their War* (New York: Harper and Row, 1987), 48. To his credit, Richardson kept his objections to FDR's decision private and went quietly into retirement.

59. Dana Priest, *The Mission: Waging War and Keeping Peace with America's Military* (New York: Norton, 2003).

60. Secretary of Defense Robert M. Gates, "Evening Lecture at the U.S. Military Academy at West Point," April 21, 2008, http://www.defenselink.mil/speeches/speech.aspx?speechid=1233.

61. On dissent by uniformed officers, see Don M. Snider, "Dissent and Strategic Leadership of the Military Profession," *Orbis* 52, no. 2 (Spring 2008): 256–77; and Leonard Wong and Douglas Lovelace, "Knowing When to Salute," *Orbis* 52, no. 2 (Spring 2008): 278–98.

62. Bryan Brown, "U.S. Special Operations Command; Meeting the Challenges of the 21st Century," *Joint Forces Quarterly* 40 (1st Quarter 2006); 39.

63. *Public Law* 99-661, 99th Congress, 2d Session (November 14, 1986).

64. Robert W. Coakley, *The Role of Federal Military Forces in Domestic Disorders, 1789–1878* (Washington, DC: United States Army Center of Military History, 1988), 83. Coakley provides the most complete history of the use of the U.S. military in a domestic role prior to passage of the Posse Comitatus Act of 1878.

65. Daniel Henninger, "Who Calls the Cavalry? The Pentagon Was Prepared for Hurricane Katrina," *Wall Street Journal*, September 9, 2005.

66. Quoted in Bill Sammon, "Bush Offers Pentagon as 'Lead Agency' in Disasters," *Washington Times*, September 26, 2005, 1.

67. The quotation from Warner is found in Mark Sappenfield, "Disaster Relief? Call in the Marines," *Christian Science Monitor*, September 19, 2005, http://www.csmonitor

.com/2005/0919/p01s01-usmi.html; see also Megan Scully, "Pentagon Begins Review of Law on Military's Domestic Role," *Government Executive*, September 27, 2005. The Warner Act passed Congress in 2006, but some provisions of the act have since been repealed.

68. Charles Dunlap, Jr., "The Origins of the Military Coup of 2012," *Parameters* 22 (Winter 1992–93): 2 –20.

69. Coakley, *Role of Federal Military Forces*, 344 (italics added).

70. Richard Kohn, "Coming Soon: A Crisis in Civil-Military Relations," *World Affairs* (Winter 2008), http://www.worldaffairsjournal.org/2008%20-%20Winter/full-civil-military.html.

71. President Barack Obama, "Remarks on a Strategy for Afghanistan and Pakistan," March 27, 2009, http://www.cfr.org/publication/18952# <http://www.cfr.org/publication/18952>.

72. Bob Woodward, "Key in Afghanistan: Economy, not Military," *Washington Post*, July 1, 2009, http://www.washingtonpost.com/wp-dyn/content/article/2009/06/30/AR2009063002811_pf.html.

73. "Obama and the General: The White House Finds a Four-Star Scapegoat for its Afghan Jitters," *Wall Street Journal*, October 7, 2009, http://online.wsj.com/article/SB10001424052970204488304574428961222276106.html.

74. See Nancy A. Youssef, "Military Growing Impatient with Obama on Afghanistan," McClatchy Washington Bureau, September 18, 2009, http://www.mcclatchydc.com/227/v-print/story/75702.html.

75. See Bob Woodward, "McChrystal: More Forces or 'Mission Failure,'" *Washington Post*, September 21, 2009, http://www.washingtonpost.com/wp-dyn/content/article/2009/09/20/AR2009092002920.html?referrer=emailarticle; and Youssef, "Military Growing Impatient."

76. See Woodward, *The War Within*.

77. For an example of this genre, see Ricardo S. Sanchez, *Wiser in Battle: A Soldier's Story* (New York: Harper, 2008).

Chapter 3: Centralization vs. Decentralization: Preparing for and Practicing Mission Command in Counterinsurgency Operations

1. Martin van Creveld, *Command in War* (Cambridge: Cambridge University Press, 1985), 268.

2. Department of the Army, Field Manual 6-0, *Mission Command: Command and Control of Army Forces*, August 2003, par. 1-67.

3. See H. R. McMaster, "Crack in the Foundation: Defense Transformation and the Underlying Assumption of Dominant Knowledge in Future War," U.S. Army War College Center for Strategic Leadership, November 2003, http://www.carlisle.army.mil/usacsl/Publications/S03-03.pdf.

4. J9 Joint Futures Lab, U.S. Joint Forces Command, "Toward a Joint Warfighting Concept: Rapid Decisive Operations," RDO Whitepaper Version 2.0, July 18, 2002, esp. 6–17; quotations are from p. 7. In his book on effects-based operations, Edward Smith stated that effects would be "cumulative over time." Edward Smith, *Effects Based Operations: Applying Network-Centric Warfare in Peace, Crisis, and War* (Washington, D.C.: CCRP, 2002), xv. See also Statement of Admiral Edmund P. Giambastiani, Jr., Commander United States Joint Forces Command, before the House Armed Services Committee, United States House of Representatives, March 12, 2003, http://usregsec.sdsu.edu/docs/AdmiralGiambastianiMarch2003.pdf.

5. Headquarters, Department of the Army, Field Manual 1, *The Army*, June 14, 2001, http://www.army.mil/features/FM1+FM2/FMIFM2.htm. Although these unrealistic assumptions were removed from the subsequent version of the manual, this thinking pervaded many army documents written between the late 1990s and 2004.

6. Steven Metz, "Insurgency and Counterinsurgency in Iraq," *Washington Quarterly* 27, no. 1 (Winter 2003): 25–36, http://www.twq.com/04winter/docs/04winter_metz.pdf.

7. Headquarters, Department of the Army, Field Manual (FM) No. 3-24, *Counterinsurgency*, December 15, 2006, p. 1-26, http://www.fas.org/irp/doddir/army/fm3-24.pdf. Hereafter cited as FM 3-24.

8. United States Air Force, "Air Force Basic Doctrine: AF Doctrine Document 1," November 17, 2003, 28, http://www.dtic.mil/doctrine/jel/service_pubs/afdd1.pdf.

9. Raymond Odierno, Nichoel Brooks, and Francesco Mastracchio, "ISR Evolution in the Iraqi Theater," *Joint Forces Quarterly* 50 (3rd Quarter 2008): 55, http://www.ndu.edu/inss/Press/jfq_pages/editions/i50/14.pdf.

10. Interview with Philip Zelikow, *Frontline*, February 6, 2007, http://www.pbs.org/wgbh/pages/frontline/endgame/themes/colonels.html.

11. On this point, see Chris Gibson, "Battlefield Victories and Strategic Success: The Path Forward in Iraq," *Military Review*, September-October 2006, 48–49, http://usacac.army.mil/CAC/milreview/English/SepOct06/Gibson.pdf.

12. Regrettably, these reconnaissance and security missions have been largely supplanted in army doctrine by "intelligence, surveillance and reconnaissance," or ISR, based in part on the belief that technology will deliver situational understanding in future war.

13. The U.S. Army counterinsurgency manual states: "Proper training addresses many possible scenarios of the COIN environment. Education should prepare Soldiers and Marines to deal with the unexpected and unknown. Senior commanders should, at a minimum, ensure that their small-unit leaders are inculcated with tactical cunning and mature judgment. Tactical cunning is the art of employing fundamental skills of the profession in shrewd and crafty ways to out-think and out-adapt enemies. Developing mature judgment and cunning requires a rigorous regimen of preparation that begins before deployment and continues throughout. *Junior leaders especially need these skills in a COIN environment because of the decentralized nature of operations* [italics added]." FM 3-24, par. 7-6.

14. This phrase was used by Colonel James B. Hickey, U.S. Army, in a conversation with the author in 2004 about how to prepare units for the demands of counterinsurgency operations.

15. David Galula, *Counterinsurgency Warfare: Theory and Practice* (Westport, CT: Praeger, 2005), 87.

16. Ibid., 88.

17. FM 3-24, p. 2-11.

18. U.S. military units preparing for operations in Afghanistan and Iraq use a variety of means to develop a basic level of cultural understanding in all soldiers. Leaders use professional reading programs; they discuss books and articles with their soldiers. Many units also use lectures and film. Excellent documentaries are available on the history of Islam as well as the history of Iraq and Afghanistan. The 2004 documentary *Voices of Iraq* proved helpful to units deploying to Iraq in 2005 because it captured so well the plight of the Iraqi people after the collapse of the Hussein regime. In 2004 the army instituted the Iraq Training Program (ITP), a self-instruction program on compact disc. The ITP was very effective: it covered Iraqi history and culture, the history of Islam, the nature of the insurgency, the United Nations program for Iraqi constitutional development and political transition, and counterinsurgency theory and doctrine. The material was tailored to three levels of responsibility: soldier, leader, and commander. Some units ensured that all soldiers completed all three levels. The army has even produced video games to develop basic knowledge of the language and culture.

19. Galula, *Counterinsurgency Warfare*, 5.

20. FM 3-24, p. 7-2.

21. Education in negotiation and mediation techniques is a gap in leaders' education that can be filled with self-study until the military begins to incorporate this instruction into its formal education programs. For relevant work conducted in this area by the Harvard Negotiation Project, see www.pon.harvard.edu/research/projects/hnp.php3. For a book that is useful in connection with preparing for negotiation and mediation in a counterinsurgency environment, see Roger Fisher and Daniel Shapiro, *Beyond Reason: Using Emotions as You Negotiate* (New York: Viking, 2005).

22. FM 3-24, p. 7-1.

23. Ibid., p. 7-2.

24. Ibid., p. 7-5.

25. Christopher Coker, *The Warrior Ethos: Military Culture and the War on Terror* (London: Routledge, 2007), 135–38.

26. For the army's values, see www.goarmy.com/life/living_the_army_values.jsp. See also Don Snider and Lloyd Mathews, eds., *The Future of the Army Profession*, rev. ed. (Boston: McGraw Hill, 2005). The counterinsurgency manual states that "the Nation's and profession's values are not negotiable" and that "violations of them are not just mistakes; they are failures in meeting the fundamental standards of the profession of arms." FM 3-24, p. 7-1.

27. Don Snider, John Nagl, and Tony Pfaff, "Army Professionalism, the Military Ethic, and Officership in the 21st Century," Strategic Studies Institute of the U.S. Army War College, 1999, www.strategicstudiesinstitute.army.mil/pdffiles/PUB282.pdf.

28. "Leaders remain aware of the emotional toll that constant combat takes on their subordinates and the potential for injuries resulting from combat stress. Such injuries can result from cumulative stress over a prolonged period, witnessing the death of a comrade, or killing other human beings. Caring leaders recognize these pressures and provide emotional 'shock absorbers' for their subordinates. Soldiers and Marines must have outlets to share their feelings and reach closure on traumatic experiences. These psychological burdens may be carried for a long time. Leaders watch for signs of possible combat stress within individuals and units." FM 3-24, p. 7-2.

29. These signs include social disconnection, distractibility, suspicion of friends, irrationality, and inconsistency. In particular, leaders look for soldiers who become "revenge driven," as they can break down the discipline of the unit and do significant damage to themselves, the mission, and their fellow soldiers.

30. Valuable books on the subject include J. Glenn Gray, *The Warriors: Reflections on Men in Battle* (New York: Harcourt Brace, 1959); Jonathan Shay, *Achilles in Vietnam: Combat Trauma and the Undoing of Character* (New York: Scribner, 1994); and David Grossman and Loren Christensen, *On Combat: The Psychology and Physiology of Deadly Conflict in War and in Peace* (IL: PPCT Research Publications, 2004).

31. As Christopher Coker observes, "The leader must help soldiers make sense of war's cruelty." Coker, *Warrior Ethos*, 20.

32. Kimberly Kagan, "III Corps AAR," unpublished paper, 2008.

33. According to Abdulkader Sinno, "Engaging in conflict consists of performing a number of essential processes, such as coordination, mobilization, and the management of information, to undermine rivals within a contested territory. Amorphous entities such as civilizations, ethnic groups, or the masses cannot perform such operations—only organizations can do so. To say that a certain conflict pits a politicized group against another is to use shorthand to indicate that organizations that recruit from among those groups are engaged in conflict." Abdulkader Sinno, *Organizations at War in Afghanistan and Beyond* (Ithaca, NY: Cornell University Press, 2008), 4.

34. Joint Publication 3.0, *Joint Operations*, September 17, 2006, xiii, xx, www.dtic.mil/doctrine.

35. FM 3-24, par. 4-16.

36. Areas of expertise include intelligence, security, security sector reform, diplomacy, international development, public finance, economics, reconstruction, rule of law, and governance.

37. Carl von Clausewitz, *On War*, ed. and trans. Michael Howard and Peter Paret (Princeton, NJ: Princeton University Press, 1976), 88–89.

38. On this point, see FM 3-24, pp. 4-4–4-5.

39. Galula, *Counterinsurgency Warfare*, 9.

40. I am indebted to Mr. Jeremy Pam of the Treasury Department, Mr. Patrick Fine of USAID, Mr. Dennis DeTray of the World Bank, and Ambassador Larry Napper of the Scowcroft Center for these ideas.

41. Galula, *Counterinsurgency Warfare*, 88.

42. Sometimes this will not be the case. For example, it might be necessary to develop large security forces quickly, which dilutes leadership and might result in undisciplined or disloyal forces that actually undermine the security situation in the long term. Senior commanders and civil authorities must identify risks in that connection and plan to reduce those risks as much as possible.

43. I am indebted to Ambassador Larry Napper for this idea.

Chapter 4: The Air Force and Twenty-First-Century Conflicts: Dysfunctional or Dynamic?

1. Quoted in Rowan Scarborough, "Pentagon Notebook," *Washington Times*, June 26, 2008, http://www.washtimes.com/news/2008/jun/26/pentagon-notebook-mcpeak-calls-mccain-too-fat/?page=2.

2. Staff Sergeant Tammie Moore, "F-15E Pilots Aid Troops Fighting in Afghanistan," *Air Force Link*, September 29, 2008, http://www.af.mil/news/story.asp?id=123117287.

3. "Air Force Adrift," *Washington Post*, June 21, 2008, http://www.washingtonpost.com/wp-dyn/content/article/2008/06/20/AR2008062002658.html.

4. "The Air Force's Tanker Mess," *New York Times*, June 29, 2008, http://www.nytimes.com/2008/06/29/opinion/29sun1.html.

5. For the ouster of the secretary and chief of staff, see Office of the Assistant Secretary of Defense (Public Affairs), "DoD News Briefing with Secretary Gates from the Pentagon," June 5, 2008, http://www.defenselink.mil/transcripts/transcript.aspx?transcriptid=4236. For the disciplining of senior leaders, see "Senior Leaders Held Accountable for Nuclear Enterprise Missteps," *Air Force Link*, September 2008, http://www.af.mil/news/story.asp?id=123116972.

6. Office of the Assistant Secretary of Defense, "Remarks to the Heritage Foundation (Colorado Springs, CO)," May 13, 2008, http://www.defenselink.mil/speeches/speech.aspx?speechid=1240.

7. For the air force's lack of influence, see for example John Tirpak, "That Missing Link," *Air Force Magazine*, October 2008, http://www.airforce-magazine.com/MagazineArchive/Documents/2008/October%202008/1008watch.pdf; Tirpak quotes former secretary of the air force Michael Wynne as saying: "We have a serious lack of Air Force influence in the Joint Staff and in the Secretariat."

8. Department of Defense, *National Defense Strategy*, June 2008, http://www.defenselink.mil/pubs/2008NationalDefenseStrategy.pdf. For a discussion of the term "irregular warfare," see William Safire, "On Language: Irregular Warfare," *New York*

Times Magazine, June 8, 2008, http://www.nytimes.com/2008/06/08/magazine/08wwln-safire-t.html.

9. Department of Defense, *National Defense Strategy*,7.

10. See, for example, Major General Robert Scales, "Clausewitz and World War IV," *The Wright Stuff*, September 4, 2008, http://www.maxwell.af.mil/au/aunews/archive/0316/Articles/Clausewitz%20and%20World%20War%20IV.pdf.

11. Headquarters, Department of the Army, Field Manual No. 3-24, *Counterinsurgency*, December 15, 2006; this document is also designated Marine Corps Warfighting Publication No. 3-33.5 and was jointly produced under the auspices of Headquarters, Marine Corps Development Command, Department of the Navy.

12. For example, see "Collateral Killing," *Washington Post*, August 31, 2008, B06, http://www.washingtonpost.com/wp-dyn/content/article/2008/08/30/AR2008083 001680_pf.html.

13. Ibid.

14. For example, see Robert Farley, "Abolish the Air Force," *American Prospect*, November 1, 2007, http://www.prospect.org/cs/articles?article=abolish_the_air_force.

15. Rebecca Grant, "Why Airmen Don't Command," *Air Force Magazine*, March 2008, http://www.airforce-magazine.com/MagazineArchive/Pages/2008/March%202008/0308command.aspx.

16. See, for example, Rebecca Grant, "The Billy Mitchell Syndrome," *Air Force Magazine*, December 2006, 52.

17. Thomas Ricks, "Petraeus Team of Warrior-PhDs," MSNBC.com, February 5, 2007, http://www.worldthreats.com/middle_east/petraeus_brain_trust.html.

18. See "Air Force Almanac," *Air Force Magazine*, May 2008, 48, http://www.airforce-magazine.com/MagazineArchive/Magazine%20Documents/2008/May%202008/0508facts_figs.pdf.

19. Michael R. Sirak, "The Wynne Outbrief," *Air Force Magazine*, September 2008, 48, http://www.airforce-magazine.com/MagazineArchive/Pages/2008/September%202008/0908wynne.aspx.

20. Colonel Tomislav S. Ruby, "Flying High, Thinking Big: The Impact of Anti-Intellectualism in the U.S. Air Force," *American Interest*, May/June 2009, 87, 88.

21. Grant, "Why Airmen Don't Command," 48 (quoting Lt. Col. Howard D. Belote).

22. Scales, "Clausewitz and World War IV."

23. Carl Builder, *The Icarus Syndrome: The Role of Air Power Theory in the Evolution and Fate of the U.S. Air Force* (New Brunswick, NJ: Transaction, 2003).

24. Ruby, "Flying High, Thinking Big," 87.

25. Ibid.

26. For a discussion of Air and Space Operations Centers, see Department of the Air Force, *Air Force Doctrine Document 2: Operations and Organization*, April 3, 2007, chapter 7, http://www.dtic.mil/doctrine/jel/service_pubs/afdd2.pdf. See also Anna Mulrine, "A Look Inside the Air Force's Control Center for Iraq and Afghanistan," *U.S. News & World Report*, May 29, 2008, ttp://www.usnews.com/articles/news/world/ 2008/05/29/a-look-inside-the-air-forces-control-center-for-iraq-and-afghanistan.html.

27. For a statement of air force doctrine, see Department of the Air Force, *Air Force Doctrine Document 2*, chapter 2. For effects-based operations, see James N. Mattis, "USJFCOM Commander's Guidance for Effects-Based Operations," *Joint Forces Quarterly* 51 (4th Quarter 2008): 105–108, http://www.ndu.edu/inss/Press/jfq_pages/editions/i51/4.pdf; and Christopher J. Castelli, "Mattis Sparks Vigorous Debate On Future Of Effects-Based Ops," InsideDefense.com, Aug. 28, 2008, http://defensenewsstand.com/insider.asp?issue=08282008sp. For a biography of General James N. Mattis, see "Gen. James. N. Mattis," United States Joint Force Command, http://www.jfcom.mil/about/mattis.htm.

28. For example, see Colonel Tomislav Z. Ruby, "Effects-Based Operations: More Important Than Ever," *Parameters* 38, no. 3 (Autumn 2008): 26–35, http://www.carlisle.army.mil/usawc/parameters/08autumn/ruby.pdf.

29. For a description of the concept of the Marine Air-Ground Task Force, see U.S. Marine Corps, *Marine Corps Concepts & Programs 2007*, 261, http://www.usmc.mil/units/hqmc/pandr/Documents/Concepts/2007/PDF/Appendicies%20CP%202007%20PDFs/CP2007AppendixA%20Pg261-267%20Marine%20Air%20Ground%20Task%20Force%20%28MAGTF%29.pdf.

30. Quoted in Castelli, "Mattis Sparks Vigorous Debate."

31. For an account of the outside review process, see Sarah Sewall, "Modernizing U.S. Counterinsurgency Practice: Rethinking Risk and Developing a National Strategy," *Military Review*, September-October 2006, http://www.ksg.harvard.edu/cchrp/Sewall%20-%20military%20review%2010_2006.pdf.

32. For example, Joe Klein writes of the document's "Zen tinge." See "When Bad Missions Happen to Good Generals," *Time*, January 22, 2007, http://www.time.com/time/magazine/article/0,9171,1576838-1,00.html.

33. Steve Coll, "The General's Dilemma," *New Yorker*, September 8, 2008, http://www.newyorker.com/reporting/2008/09/08/080908fa_fact_coll?currentPage=all.

34. Samantha Power, "Our War on Terror," *New York Times*, July 29, 2007, http://select.nytimes.com/preview/2007/07/29/books/1154682945065.html.

35. For more on this point, see Charles J. Dunlap, Jr., "Making Revolutionary Change: Airpower in COIN Today," *Parameters* 38, no. 2 (Summer 2008), http://www.carlisle.army.mil/USAWC/parameters/08summer/dunlap.pdf.

36. Quoted in Charles M. Sennot, "The Good Soldier," *Men's Journal*, June 2008, http://www.mensjournal.com/the-good-soldier.

37. "Link Hard, Soft Power," *Defense News*, September 8, 2008, http://www.defensenews.com/story.php?i=3712849.

38. For the increase in air strikes, see for example Anthony H. Cordesman, "US Airpower in Iraq and Afghanistan: 2004–2007," Center for Strategic and International Studies, December 13, 2007, http://www.csis.org/media/csis/pubs/071213_oif-oef_airpower.pdf.

39. Michael M. Dunn, "The Pile-On Effect," Air Force Association, July 9, 2008, http://www.afa.org/EdOp/edop_7-10-08.asp.

40. Josh White, "Overlooked Air Force Launches Ads," *Washington Post*, February 25, 2008, http://www.washingtonpost.com/wp-dyn/content/article/2008/02/24/AR2008022402083.html.

41. Thomas Ricks, *Fiasco* (New York: Penguin Press, 2006).

42. See Staff Sergeant J. G. Buzanowski, "Air Force is 'Above All,'" Secretary of the Air Force Public Affairs, February 20, 2008, http://www.af.mil/news/story.asp?id=123087033; and Lisa Burgess et al., "Mixed Reviews for New Air Force Slogan," *Stars and Stripes*, February 29, 2008, http://www.military.com/features/0,15240,163068,00. html.

43. Winslow T. Wheeler, "An Air Force in Free Fall," *Counterpunch*, July 23, 2008, http://www.counterpunch.org/wheeler07232008.html.

44. John Hendren, cited in Dr. Donald P. Wright and Colonel Timothy R. Reese (with others), *On Point II,* United States Army Combined Arms Center, 2008, 295, http://usacac.army.mil/CAC2/CSI/OnPointII.pdf.

45. Ibid. (emphasis added).

46. See William M. Arkin, "Shock and Awe Worked, God Help Us," Early Warning (Washingtonpost.com), March 19, 2007, http://huzmidlan.blogspot.com/2007/03/shock-and-awe-worked-god-help-us.html.

47. Michael Donley, "A Time of Transition" (speech, Air Force Association's 24th Annual Air & Space Conference and Technology Exposition, Washington, D.C., September 15, 2008), http://www.af.mil/library/speeches/speech.asp?id=400.

48. James E. Baker, "LBJ's Ghost: A Contextual Approach to Targeting Decisions and the Commander in Chief," *Chicago Journal of International Law* (October 2003): 417.

49. See Secretary of Defense Robert Gates, Office of the Assistant Secretary of Defense (Public Affairs), Opening Statement to the House Armed Services Committee, September 10, 2008, http://www.defenselink.mil/speeches/speech.aspx?speechid= 1272.

50. Richard K. Betts, "A Disciplined Defense," *Foreign Affairs* 86, no. 6 (November/December 2007), http://www.realclearpolitics.com/articles/2007/11/a_disciplined_defense.html.

51. Ibid.

52. See Tom Vanden Brook, "Pentagon: New MRAPs Saving Troops' Lives," *USA Today*, April 4, 2008, http://www.usatoday.com/news/military/2008-04-03-MRAPs_N.htm.

53. General Barry R. McCaffrey, "Memorandum for Colonel Mike Meese, United States Military Academy, Subject: After Action Report," B. R. McCaffrey Associates LLC, October 15, 2007, http://www.mccaffreyassociates.com/pages/documents/AirForceAAR-101207.pdf. For information on the weapons mentioned, see "MQ-1 Predator Unmanned Aerial Vehicle," Department of the Air Force Factsheet, September 2008, http://www.af.mil/factsheets/factsheet.asp?fsID=122; "MQ9 Reaper Unmanned Aerial Vehicle," Department of the Air Force Factsheet, September 2008, http://www.af.mil/factsheets/factsheet.asp?fsID=6405; and "RQ-4A/B Global Hawk High-Altitude, Long-Endurance, Unmanned Reconnaissance Aircraft," SPG Media Limited, 2008, http://www.airforce-technology.com/projects/global/.

54. For example, see Major Jon Huss, "Exploiting the Psychological Effects of Airpower," *Aerospace Power Journal*, Winter 1999, 23, http://www.airpower.maxwell. af.mil/airchronicles/apj/apj99/win99/huss.htm.

55. See Josh White, "U.S. Boosts Its Use of Airstrikes in Iraq," *Washington Post*, January 17, 2008, http://www.washingtonpost.com/wp-dyn/content/article/2008/01/16/AR2008011604148.html.

56. General Tommy Franks, *American Soldier* (New York: Regan Books, 2004), 312 (emphasis added).

57. Juan Forero, "Colombia's Rebels Face Possibility of Implosion," *Washington Post*, March 22, 2008, http://www.washingtonpost.com/wp-dyn/content/article/2008/03/21/AR2008032103536_pf.html.

58. John Barry and Evan Thomas, "Up in the Sky, An Unblinking Eye," *Newsweek*, June 9, 2008, http://www.newsweek.com/id/139432.

59. Compare J. B. Glubb, who observed that British air operations in the colonial wars of the early twentieth century may not have caused much physical damage to adversaries, but that "their tremendous moral effect is largely due to the demoralization engendered in the tribesman by his *feelings of helplessness and his inability to reply effectively to the attack.*" J. B. Glubb, "Air and Ground Forces in Punitive Expeditions," *RUSI Journal* (August 1926): 782; quoted in Major Michael A. Longoria, "A Historical View of Air Policing: Lessons from the British Experience between the Wars, 1919–1939" (thesis, School of Advanced Airpower Studies, Air University, June 1993), 23, http://www.au.af.mil/au/aul/aupress/saas_Theses/SAASS_Out/Longoria/ longoria.pdf.

60. For example, civilian deaths caused by ground fire are described in M. Karim Faiez and Laura King, "3 Afghan Children Killed in Western Artillery Strike," *Los Angeles Times*, September 2, 2008, http://www.latimes.com/news/nationworld/world/la-fg-afghan2-2008sep02,0,2374381.story.

61. For example, see Cabin Maurer, "Taliban show media savvy," FayObserver.com, January 12, 2008, http://www.fayobserver.com/article?id=282842.

62. Brigadier General Richard Blanchette, quoted in Pamela Constable, "A Modernized Taliban Thrives in Afghanistan," *Washington Post*, September 20, 2008.

63. Ibid.

64. General David D. McKiernan, quoted in Jim Garamone, "Secretary Gates examines close-air support at Bagram," *American Forces Press Service*, September 18, 2008, http://www.af.mil/news/story_print.asp?id=123115773.

65. For NATO's reluctance to incur civilian casualties, see Noor Kahn, "Afghan Civilians Said Killed in Clash," Yahoo! News, June 30, 2007, http://news.yahoo. com/s/ap/20070630/ap_on_re_as/afghanistan. See also Pamela Constable, "NATO Hopes to Undercut Taliban with 'Surge' of Projects," *Washington Post*, September 27, 2008, http://www.washingtonpost.com/wp-dyn/content/article/2008/09/26/AR2008 092603452_pf.html, quoting Brigadier General Richard Blanchette, chief spokesman for NATO forces, as saying "If there is the likelihood of even one civilian casualty, we will not strike, not even if we think Osama bin Laden is down there."

66. "Protocol Additional to the Geneva Conventions of August 12, 1949, and Relating to the Protection of Victims of International Armed Conflicts (Protocol I), December 12, 1977," art. 57, para 2(b), 1125 U.N.T.S. 3 (entered into force December 7, 1978). Although the United States is not a party to Protocol I, military lawyers often refer to it for guidance, and parts of it are considered customary international law.

67. See Charles J. Dunlap, Jr., "Lawfare amid Warfare," *Washington Times*, August 3, 2007, http://washingtontimes.com/article/20070803/EDITORIAL/108030004/1013.

68. Human Rights Watch, *Troops in Contact: Airstrikes and Civilian Deaths in Afghanistan* (New York: Human Rights Watch, 2008), 29, http://hrw.org/reports/2008/afghanistan0908/afghanistan0908web.pdf.

69. Anna Mulrine, "A Look Inside the Air Force's Command and Control Center for Iraq and Afghanistan," *U.S. News & World Report*, May 29, 2008, http://www.usnews.com/articles/news/world/2008/05/29/a-look-inside-the-air-forces-control-center-for-iraq-and-afghanistan.html.

70. Marc Garlasoc, quoted by Josh White, "The Man on Both Sides of Air War Debate," *Washington Post*, February 13, 2008, http://www.washingtonpost.com/wp-dyn/content/article/2008/02/12/AR2008021202692.html.

71. General James Conway, quoted in Mark Thompson, "Collateral Tragedies," *Time*, September 4, 2008, http://www.time.com/time/magazine/article/0,9171,1838778,00.html.

72. Ibid.

73. See, for example, Charles J. Dunlap, Jr., "Using Bad PR is Taliban Defense Against Airpower," *Atlanta Journal-Constitution*, September 17, 2008, http://www.ajc.com/opinion/content/opinion/stories/2008/09/17/dunlaped_0917.html.

74. FM 3-24, par. 1-67.

75. Bob Woodward, "Why Did Violence Plummet? It Wasn't Just the Surge," *Washington Post*, Sept. 8, 2008, A9, http://www.washingtonpost.com/wp-dyn/content/article/2008/09/07/AR2008090701847.html. See also Bob Woodward, *The War Within: A Secret White House History, 2006–2008* (New York: Simon and Schuster, 2008).

76. William R. Polk, *Violent Politics: A History of Insurgency, Terrorism & Guerrilla War, From the American Revolution to Iraq* (New York: HarperCollins, 2007), xvi.

77. See Zbigniew Brzezinski, "The Smart Way Out of a Foolish War," *Washington Post*, March 30, 2008, http://www.washingtonpost.com/wp-dyn/content/article/2008/03/27/AR2008032702405_pf.html: "It is also important to recognize that most of the anti-U.S. insurgency in Iraq has not been inspired by al-Qaeda. Locally based jihadist groups have gained strength only insofar as they have been able to identify themselves with the fight against a hated foreign occupier."

78. Mark Benjamin, "Killing 'Bubba' From the Skies," Salon.com, February 15, 2008, http://www.salon.com/news/feature/2008/02/15/air_war/.

79. Laura King, "In Afghanistan, Insurgents Attacking Cellphone Network," *Los Angeles Times*, April. 23, 2008, http://www.latimes.com/news/nationworld/world/la-fg-cellphones23apr23,1,3026509.story.

80. James S. Corum, *Bad Strategies: How Major Powers Fail in Counterinsurgency* (Osceola, WI: Zenith Press, 2008), 238.

81. CNN/Opinion Research Corporation Poll. August 29–31, 2008, cited in "Iraq," PollingReport.com, http://www.pollingreport.com/iraq.htm.

82. See Lieutenant General Tom McInerney, USAF (Ret.), "Budgeting for the Joint Force," Human Events.com, February 9, 2007, http://www.humanevents.com/article.php?id=19352.

83. See U.S. Department of Defense, *Unmanned Systems Roadmap 2007–2032*, December 10, 2007, http://www.acq.osd.mil/usd/Unmanned%20Systems%20Roadmap.2007-2032.pdf.

84. Thom Shanker, "At Odds with the Air Force, Army Adds Its Own Aviation Unit," *New York Times*, June 22, 2008, http://www.nytimes.com/2008/06/22/washington/22military.html.

85. Yochi J. Dreazen, "U.S. to Expand Drone Use, Other Surveillance in Afghanistan," *Wall Street Journal*, September 18, 2008.

86. Headquarters United States Air Force, *Operation Anaconda: An Air Power Perspective*, February 7, 2005, 114, http://www.af.mil/shared/media/document/AFD-060726-037.pdf.

87. Greg Grant, "U.S. Cuts Role of Apache for Deep Attack," *Defense News*, April 3, 2006, http://www.defensenews.com/story.php?F=1607858&C=airwar. For background on the Apache helicopter, see Department of the Army, *Apache Longbow*, Army Fact File, http://www.army.mil/factfiles/equipment/aircraft/apache.html.

88. Major Robert J. Seifert, "Iraq and the AC-130: Gunships Unleashed," *Joint Forces Quarterly* 45 (2nd quarter 2007): 78–83, http://www.ndu.edu/inss/Press/jfq_pages/editions/i45/19.pdf.

89. Ibid., 79.

90. Lieutenant General Michael Vane, "An Underfunded 'Precision Weapon,'" *Defense News*, May 26, 2008.

91. Lieutenant General Raymond T. Odierno et al., "ISR in the Iraqi Theater," *Joint Forces Quarterly* (3rd quarter 2008): 51–55, http://www.ndu.edu/inss/Press/jfq_pages/editions/i50/14.pdf.

92. Matthew Cox and Gina Cavallaro, "Petraeus: ISR Gear is Key to Success," *Army Times*, April 11, 2008, http://www.armytimes.com/news/2008/04/military_petraeus_gear_042108/.

93. See Dunn, "Pile-On Effect."

94. Ibid.

95. General Norton Schwartz, "AFA Convention Keynote," September 16, 2008, http://www.af.mil/shared/media/document/AFD-080916-083.pdf .

96. Colin S. Gray, *The Airpower Advantage in Future Warfare* (Maxwell Air Force Base, AL: Air University, 2007), 32, http://aupress.maxwell.af.mil/ARI_Papers/ GrayARI2.pdf. For criticisms of high-tech weapons, see, for example, Ann Scott Tyson, "Gates Criticizes Conventional Focus at the Start of Iraq War," *Washington Post*, September 30, 2008, A4.

97. Donley, "Time of Transition."

Chapter 5: Strategy, Counterinsurgency, and the Army

1. Colonel David Maxwell, U.S. Army, e-mail message to the author, April 7, 2008.

2. Walter B. Wriston, *The Twilight of Sovereignty: How the Information Revolution is Transforming Our World* (New York: Replica, 1997).

3. Historically, a third qualifier—that U.S. commitment is kept low—would seem to apply, since successful counterinsurgency campaigns appear to be small; El Salvador and Colombia are good examples. But U.S. operations in Iraq may eventually prove an example of a successful large counterinsurgency campaign.

4. There are many study groups and commissions now making recommendations on restoring both military assistance and the State Department's strength and authority. A succinct overview can be found in Department of Defense, *The Country Team in American Strategy* (Washington, D.C.: Department of Defense, Office of Force Transformation, December 2006).

5. Colonel David Galula, *Counterinsurgency Warfare: Theory and Practice* (Westport, CT: Praeger, 2006), 90.

6. U.S. Army and Marine Corps, *U.S. Army/Marine Corps Counterinsurgency Field Manual* (FM 3-24, MCWP 3-33.5): (Chicago: University of Chicago Press, 2007), 39.

7. The exact wording is: "Now one word about your relations to the military. As you know, the United States Diplomatic Mission includes Service Attaches, Military Assistance Advisory Groups and other Military components attached to the Mission. It does not, however, include United States military forces operating in the field where such forces are under the command of a United States area military commander. The line of authority runs from me, to the Secretary of Defense, to the Joint Chiefs of Staff in Washington and to the area commander in the field." President John F. Kennedy, "Memorandum from the President to the Heads of Executive Departments and Agencies," White House, May 29, 1961, quoted in Robert B. Killebrew et al., *The Country Team in American Strategy* (Washington, D.C.: U.S. Department of Defense, 2006), app. A, 51.

8. Quoted in Killebrew et al., *Country Team in American Strategy*, frontispiece.

9. Frank Hoffman, *Conflict in the 21st Century: The Rise of Hybrid Wars* (Arlington, VA: Potomac Institute for Policy Studies, 2007), 29.

10. This is already occurring in the U.S. Southern Command and the new U.S. Africa Command, both in areas where direct U.S. combat action is unlikely.

11. For example, see Department of Defense, *The Country Team in American Strategy*; and Council of Foreign Relations and Center for Strategic and International Studies, *Task Force Report: State Department Reform* (New York: Council on Foreign Relations, 2001).

12. Hezbollah forces opposing the Israeli offensive in the summer of 2006 were equipped with high-tech fiber-optic communications networks and command-and-control systems fully as modern as those employed by the Israelis.

13. For example, the current president of Rwanda, Paul Kagame, was a student at the army's Command and General Staff College.

Index

About the Authors

Thomas Donnelly is a resident fellow in defense and security policy studies and the director of the Center for Defense Studies at AEI. He is the author, with Frederick W. Kagan, of *Ground Truth: The Future of U.S. Land Power* (AEI Press, May 2008); the coeditor, with Gary J. Schmitt, of *Of Men and Materiel: The Crisis in Military Resources* (AEI Press, 2007); and the author of *The Military We Need* (AEI Press, 2005), *Operation Iraqi Freedom: A Strategic Assessment* (AEI Press, 2004), and several other books. From 1995 to 1999, he was policy group director and a professional staff member for the House Armed Services Committee. Mr. Donnelly also served as a member of the U.S.-China Economic and Security Review Commission. He is a former editor of *Armed Forces Journal*, *Army Times*, and *Defense News*.

Major General Charles J. Dunlap, Jr., is deputy judge advocate general at Head-quarters U.S. Air Force, where he assists in professional oversight of more than 2,200 judge advocates, 350 civilian attorneys, 1,400 enlisted para-legals, and 500 civilians worldwide. In addition to overseeing an array of military justice, operational, international, and civil law functions, General Dunlap provides legal advice to the Air Staff and commanders at all levels. He has served in the United Kingdom and Korea and deployed in support of vari-ous operations in the Middle East and Africa, including operations Iraqi Freedom and Enduring Freedom. General Dunlap has led military delegations to Uruguay, the Czech Republic, South Africa, Colombia, and Iraq. Prior to assuming his current position, General Dunlap served as the staff judge advocate at Headquarters Air Command.

Peter D. Feaver is a professor of political science at Duke University. From 2005 to 2007, he was special advisor for strategic planning and institutional reform on the National Security Council staff at the White House. From 1993 to 1994, Professor Feaver served as director for defense policy and arms control on the National Security Council, where his responsibilities included counterproliferation policy, national security strategy review, regional nuclear arms control, and other defense policy issues. In addition to numerous articles on American foreign policy, nuclear proliferation, information warfare, and U.S. national security, Professor Feaver is author of *Armed Servants: Agency, Oversight, and Civil-Military Relations* (Harvard University Press, 2003), and coauthor of *Paying the Human Costs of War* (Princeton University Press, 2009).

Frederick W. Kagan is a resident scholar and the director of the Critical Threats Project at AEI. He served as an advisor to General Stanley A. McChrystal in 2009. His most recent reports, based on multiple trips to Afghanistan, focus on force requirements and analyses of how various stakeholders in Afghanistan and Pakistan would respond to different U.S. policy scenarios. Mr. Kagan is the author of *Choosing Victory: A Plan for Success in Iraq*, the first of four reports by the Iraq Planning Group at AEI. His most recent book, *Ground Truth: The Future of U.S. Land Power*, coauthored with Thomas Donnelly, was released in 2008 by the AEI Press. In 2006, he published *End of the Old Order: Napoleon and Europe, 1801–1805* (De Capo Books) and *Finding the Target: The Transformation of American Military Policy* (Encounter Books). Mr. Kagan was previously an associate professor of military history at the U.S. Military Academy at West Point. A contributing editor at the *Weekly Standard*, he has written numerous articles on defense and foreign policy issues for *Foreign Affairs*, *Wall Street Journal*, *Washington Post*, *Los Angeles Times*, and *New York Times*, among other periodicals.

Colonel Robert Killebrew is a private consultant in national defense issues. He is a retired army infantry colonel who served in the U.S. Army Special Forces and airborne units. While on active duty, he inaugurated the "Army After Next" project that became the army transformation war-game series. Since retirement, he has served on the U.S. Commission on National Security/21st Century (the Hart-Rudman Commission), and has contributed to other Department of Defense and private studies of national defense issues. Colonel Killebrew has written extensively in a variety of publications on emerging defense issues and taught national and military strategy at the U.S. Army War College. He is now a senior fellow at the Center for a New American Security.

Brigadier General H. R. McMaster is director of Concept Development and Learning at the U.S. Army Training and Doctrine Command. He is the author of *Dereliction of Duty: Lyndon Johnson, Robert McNamara, the Joint Chiefs of Staff, and the Lies that Led to Vietnam* (HarperCollins, 1997) and numerous articles and monographs on military history and defense affairs. Brigadier General McMaster holds a PhD in history from the University of North Carolina at Chapel Hill, is a senior consulting fellow at the International Institute for Strategic Studies, a research fellow at the Hoover Institution, and a member of the Council on Foreign Relations. He served as special assistant to Commander, Multinational Force-Iraq from January 2007 until May 2008. From June 2004 until June 2006, he served as the seventy-first colonel of the Third Armored Cavalry Regiment. He joined U.S. Central Command in May 2003 and served as director of the Commander's Advisory Group until May 2004. Brigadier General McMaster was an assistant professor of history at the U.S. Military Academy at West Point from 1994 to 1996.

Mackubin Thomas Owens is associate dean of academics for electives and directed research and professor of national security affairs at the Naval War College in Newport, Rhode Island, and editor of *Orbis*, the quarterly journal of the Foreign Policy Research Institute (FPRI). From 1990 to 1997, he was editor-in-chief of the quarterly defense journal *Strategic Review* and adjunct professor of international relations at Boston University. Before joining the faculty of the Naval War College, he served as national security advisor to Senator Bob Kasten (R-Wisc.) and director of legislative affairs for the nuclear weapons programs of the Department of Energy during the Reagan administration. Professor Owens is an adjunct fellow at the Ashbrook Center for Public Affairs at Ashbrook University and has served as a consultant to the Strategy and Plans Division of Headquarters Marine Corps, the J-5 Strategy, and the Joint Staff.